Giovanni Previdi

THE ART OF HAT-MAKING

ITALIAN CRAFTSMANSHIP FROM THE CERVO VALLEY

new Heroes & Pioneers

To Lucia, my mother

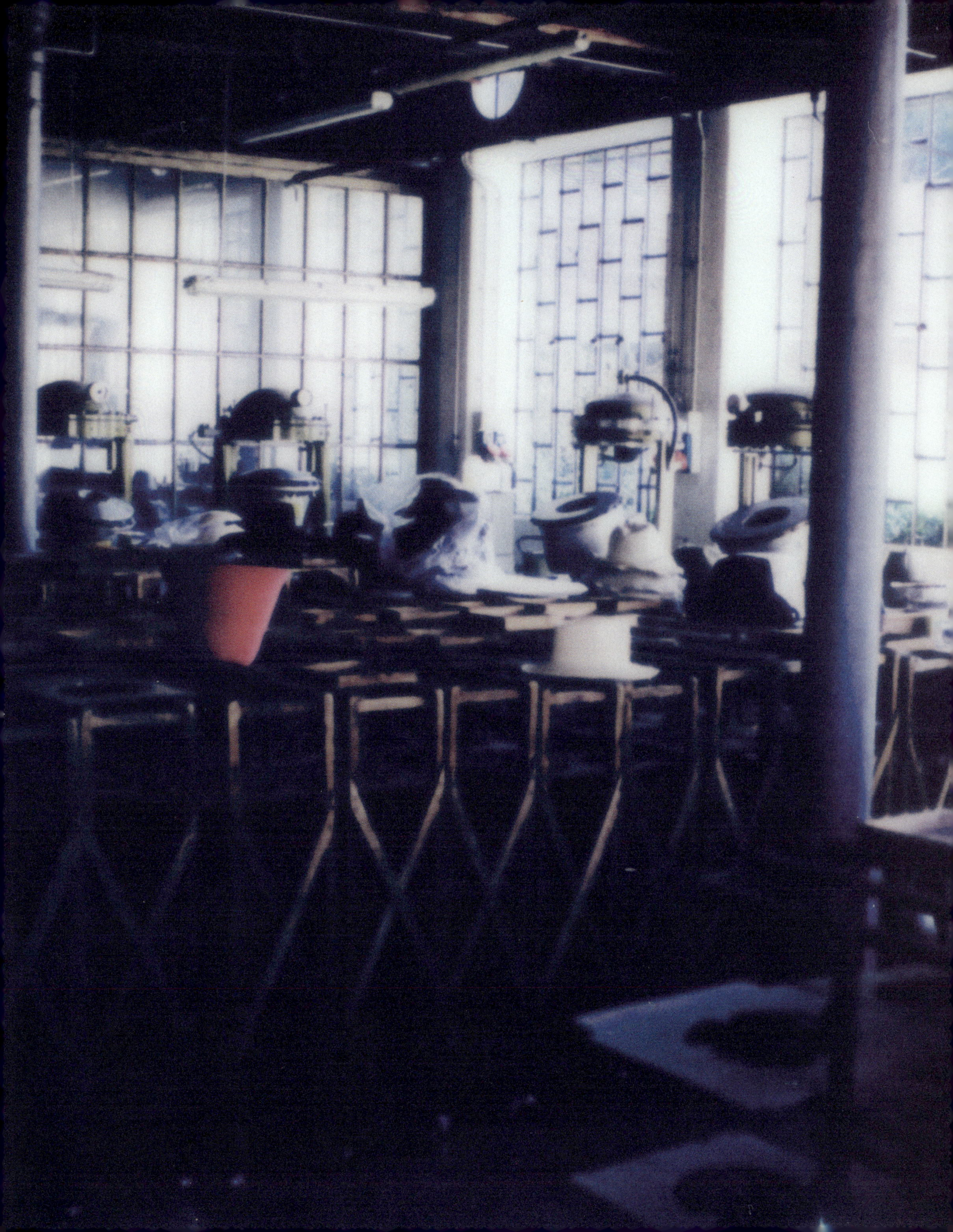

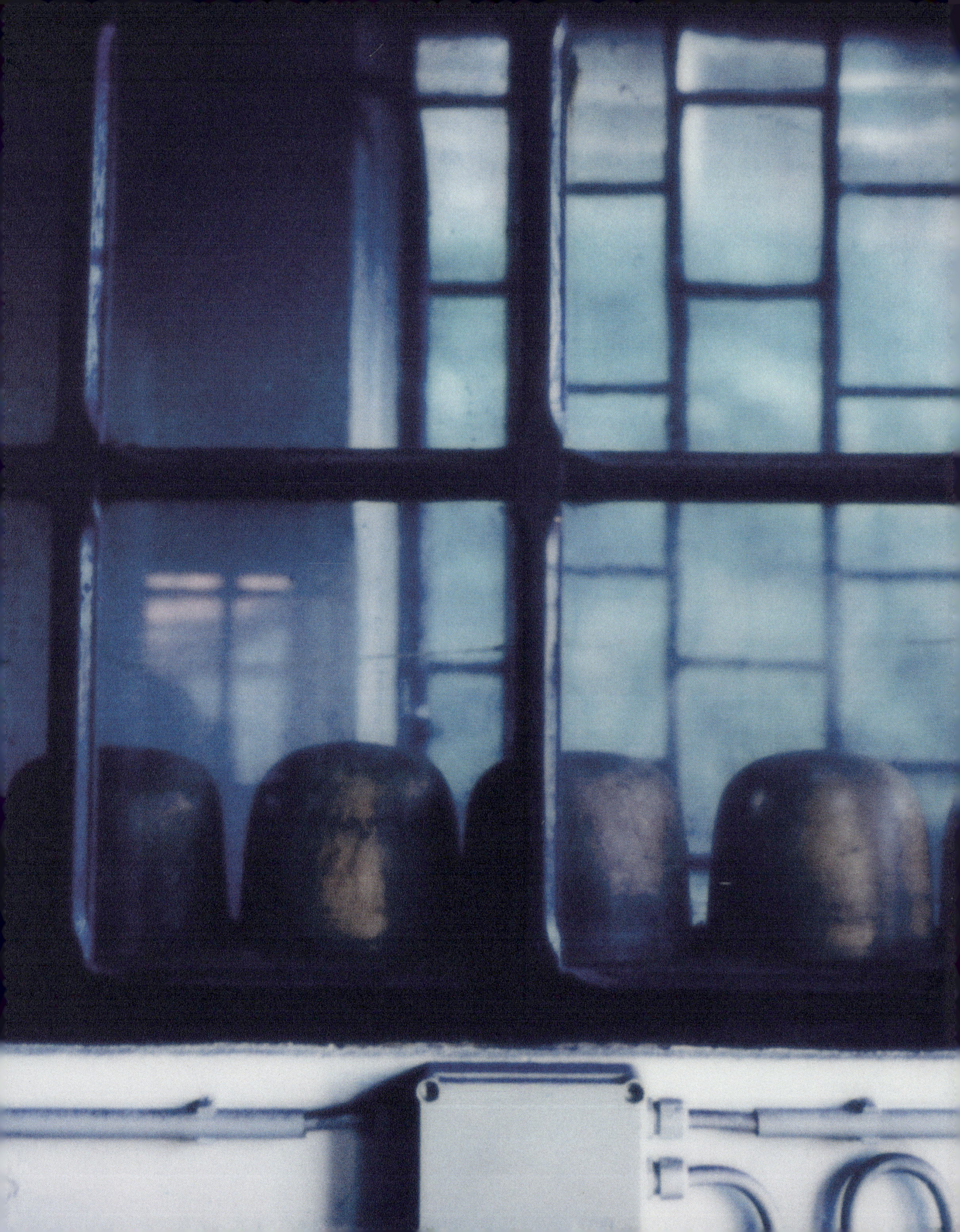

THE DISCOVERY OF A FORGOTTEN CRAFT IN THE VALLEY OF WATER

In the Piedmont region, in Sagliano Micca, there is a long, narrow valley — shady and cool in summer, dark and icy in winter. In this glimpse of the Alps, before the road becomes steep and gets lost among the chestnut and ash trees, stands the Cappellificio Cervo, there sincefirst established in 1897.

One morning in November 2019, I find myself in these parts once again. Attracted by the tall chimney that towers above the factory and driven by my curiosity as to whether hats are still being made there, I decide to knock on the door. In my backpack, I'm carrying my Polaroid SX-70.

A very tall man dressed in a long, blue, well-buttoned shirt and, needless to say, a wide-brimmed hat on his head, opens the door. Two pens in his breast pocket, glasses on his nose. The pleasantries are very quick. Giorgio Borrione — that's the name of the last master hatter — loudly calls for a certain Benedetta, then disappears behind the door. Next thing I know, I find myself standing in front of his daughter, who is as tall as he is. I feel small. *Now, what do I tell her?*, I think to myself. *What am I really doing here, at the hat factory?*

Benedetta invites me in. We chat in the 'outlet' room and I begin to learn about the history of this magical, timeless place that, inevitably, summons childhood memories in those who visit it — assuming they know Lewis Carroll's 'The Mad Hatter', that is.

I discover that this is the birthplace of the official hat of the Alpini, the Italian Army; that the American director Spike Lee wore a hat made by these hatters at the last Cannes Film Festival, one that was made in just two days; and that, the stylist of a prestigious international fashion brand could enter through the same door I did, at any given moment. Paris, Milan, Sagliano Micca: it's a small world, indeed.

Wooden hat blocks (opposite page)
Laboratory (previous spread)

After about half an hour, the conversation draws to a close. I have listened to endless stories and curious anecdotes about the Cervo hat factory, but the risk of leaving without having actually seen it becomes more and more evident. Beneath where I am standing, just one floor down, I imagine hats coming to life. I learn that there is not a single seam in a hat: dome and brim are one body.

Not without effort, I must admit, I convince Benedetta to show me the factory. Within thirty seconds, I am finally engulfed in a historic space of origin and creation.

Soft blades of light pour in through large windows, one of which has been left open to welcome the distinct gurgling of a stream. Everything here is called 'deer': the hat factory, the valley and even the stream.

The hatmakers are silently at work, their heads bent over a scrap of felt, a spool of coloured thread or a decorative ribbon. Their hands move through archaic gestures, precise and confident. It is as if they are driven by instinct, and I fear that my presence might break this spell of perfect harmony in unison, but fortunately this is not the case.

In fact, Francesco, the quality control officer, looks up and greets me as his hands continue to brush a burgundy-coloured hat, following the direction of the fabric, until even the smallest unwanted residue has been removed. Then he hands the hat to Giorgio, who trims the brim with scissors, cuts off the excess felt, and studies it with professional attention before placing it in a wooden cage along with all the others. This cage is placed on the hoist that will take it straight to the ground floor where master seamstresses will apply the garniture or simply the size labels.

The final touch is up to the women, and one mistake would undo days and days of work. The sound of a radio playing a summer hit keeps them company and lends rhythm to these precious, refined movements that seem like a blessing of sorts, sending the hats off on their way to shop windows in Rome, New York or London. Soon after, the hats arrive at the warehouse for packing and shipping.

I am tempted to pull the Polaroid camera out of my backpack but don't do it for fear of being intrusive.

Benedetta answers a phone call. I wander freely around the hat factory. All around me are dozens and dozens of hat forms made of both wood and aluminum, all neatly arranged on visible shelves. Each one is marked with a name that identifies it and makes it as unique as the hat to which it will give shape. My eyes rest on three of them: "Aramis", "Ford" and, finally, "Diplomatico" (also known as "Homburg"), which I learn was the hat worn by none other than Sir Winston Churchill.

But how is a hat made?

The 'capelina', a semi-finished product previously passed through the steaming department, is placed on top of these forms. At this point, heavy sandbags are slowly lowered onto them so that the felt adheres to the chosen shape. The shaping is perfect. Et voilà — a hat in its initial stage but already a hat in its own right, ready for finishing. Behind such seemingly simple, mechanical and repetitive gestures lie the mistakes, achievements and technical knowledge of several generations of hat makers.

Giorgio, whom I cross paths with several times during my tour of the factory, tells me that the search for new and more innovative materials of natural origin is continuous. Most importantly, however, it must respect the peculiarities of felt, such as water repellency and breathability.

The visit continues, with every step I find myself captivated by hundreds of objects, some of which I have never seen before and which I could hardly describe other than with a photograph. Start and stop buttons, blowing machines that separate impurities from fur, giant tanks used to dye felt and a myriad of different tools ranging from hammers, tweezers and brushes with metal bristles to scissors, screwdrivers, bolts, cans of lubricant, sandpaper and irons. The list could go on and on. There is also Pimpa, a cute dachshund who leaps out of his kennel and comes to sniff my shoes.

As I am about to leave, the doorbell rings. A long-term customer of the hat factory enters and asks whether his 25-year-old hat can be fixed on the fly. While Benedetta replaces its frieze, the gentleman speaks of it as though it were and old friend, says he never leaves the house without first putting it on his head and that, on rainy days it is better than an umbrella, not one drop seeps through.

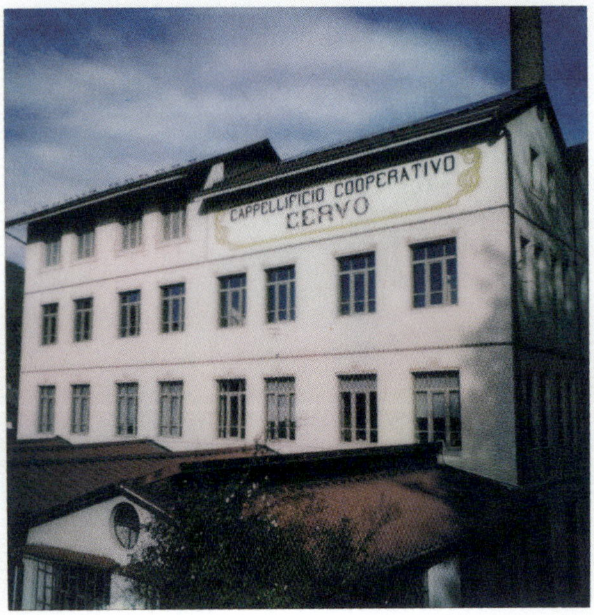
CAPPELLIFICIO COOPERATIVO
CERVO

What is striking about each and every one of these handmade hats is their durability. Even the most used hats, turn out as good as new when given the proper care. I understand that behind every quality production there is an important concept that contributes to the health of our planet: reuse. And it is clear that only objects that are made and designed to last can be reused. The rest is disposable, pollution. If it is true that many small acts can save a planet already at the end of its tethers, buying much less but better is one of them.

The gentleman waves goodbye and leaves with his hat pulled back on.
On a wall near the exit hangs a black and white photograph from a long time ago, perhaps the 1950s. It shows a huge square packed with hundreds of people and of all of them only one stands out: the only one not wearing a hat. Today things have changed. If we took that same photograph tomorrow, we would be struck by the exact opposite. Cappellificio Cervo — which has recently been acquired by the Ermenegildo Zegna Group — aims to bring this once indispensable object back into the contemporary world. To do this requires not a time machine but quality, sustainability and communicational strategies.

Then Covid arrives but even through that demoralising period I can't get the hats out of my head. Two years later, as soon as the pandemic situation improves and the restrictions are relaxed, I phone Benedetta. I've been thinking about it for a long time, I tell her, why don't we do a photo book on the hat factory? I was thinking of using my Polaroid SX-70, the one Andy Warhol used too. An analogue camera from 50 years ago, instant photography — we can try it and see what comes out. The Borrione family is enthusiastic and the Ermenegildo Zegna Group approves the project.

Some time later, and on several occasions, I find myself shooting elbow to elbow with the hatters, witnessing a small fraction of the high-level craftsmanship that can be found in many tiny villages throughout Italy, tucked away from the coasts of mass tourism. This book is meant to be a tangible testimony (ode to is perfect) of that. And so, I continue to wander freely around the factory, trying to compose a story that illustrate even just a small part of the astonishing art of making a hat in images.

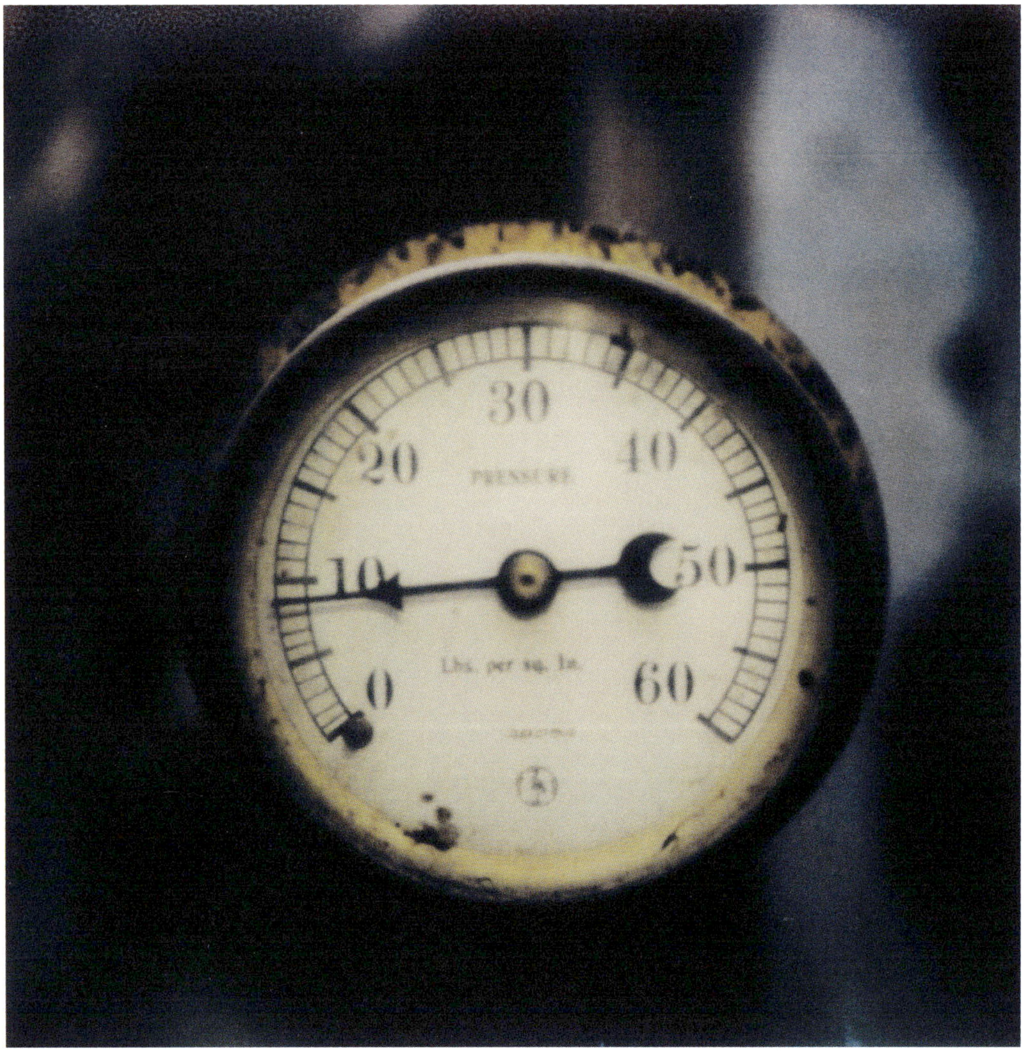

Manometer

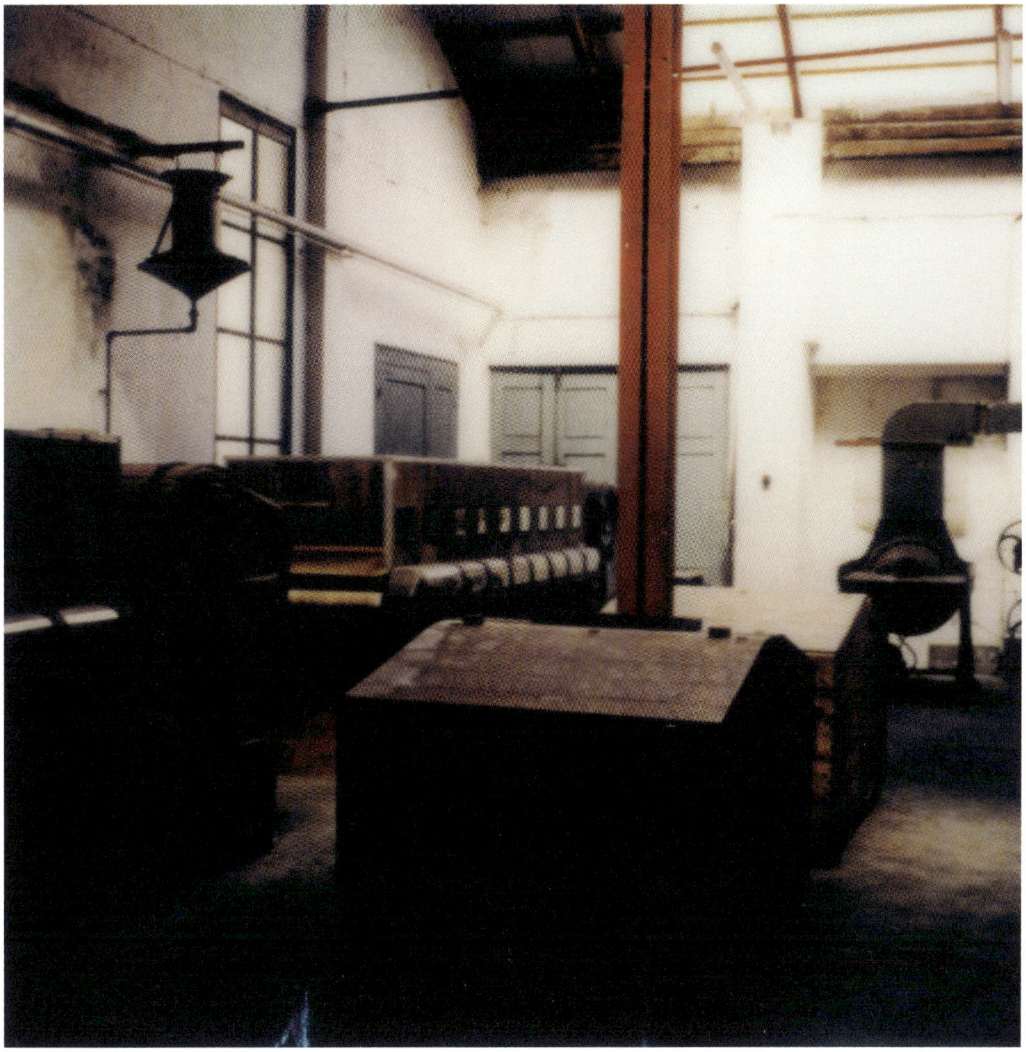

Blow molding machines

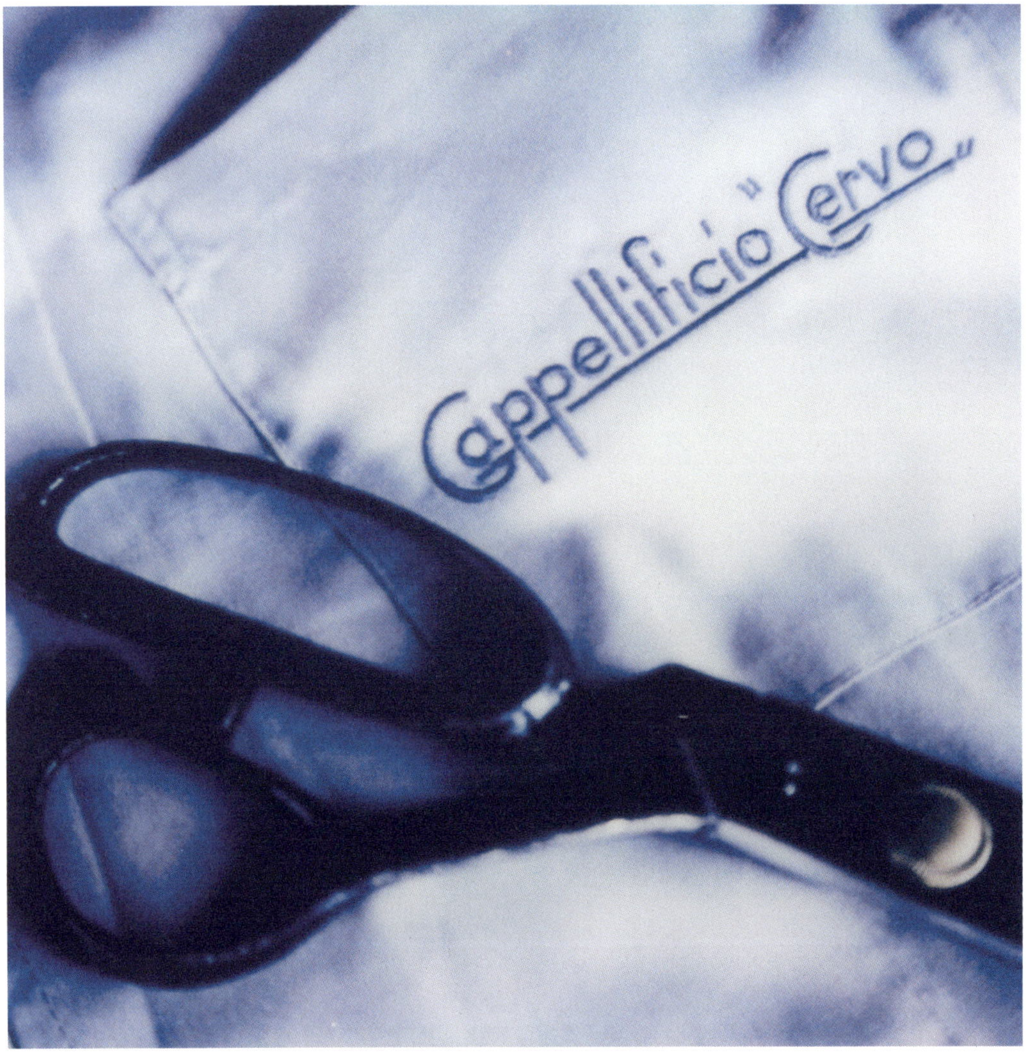

Cappellificio Cervo scissors

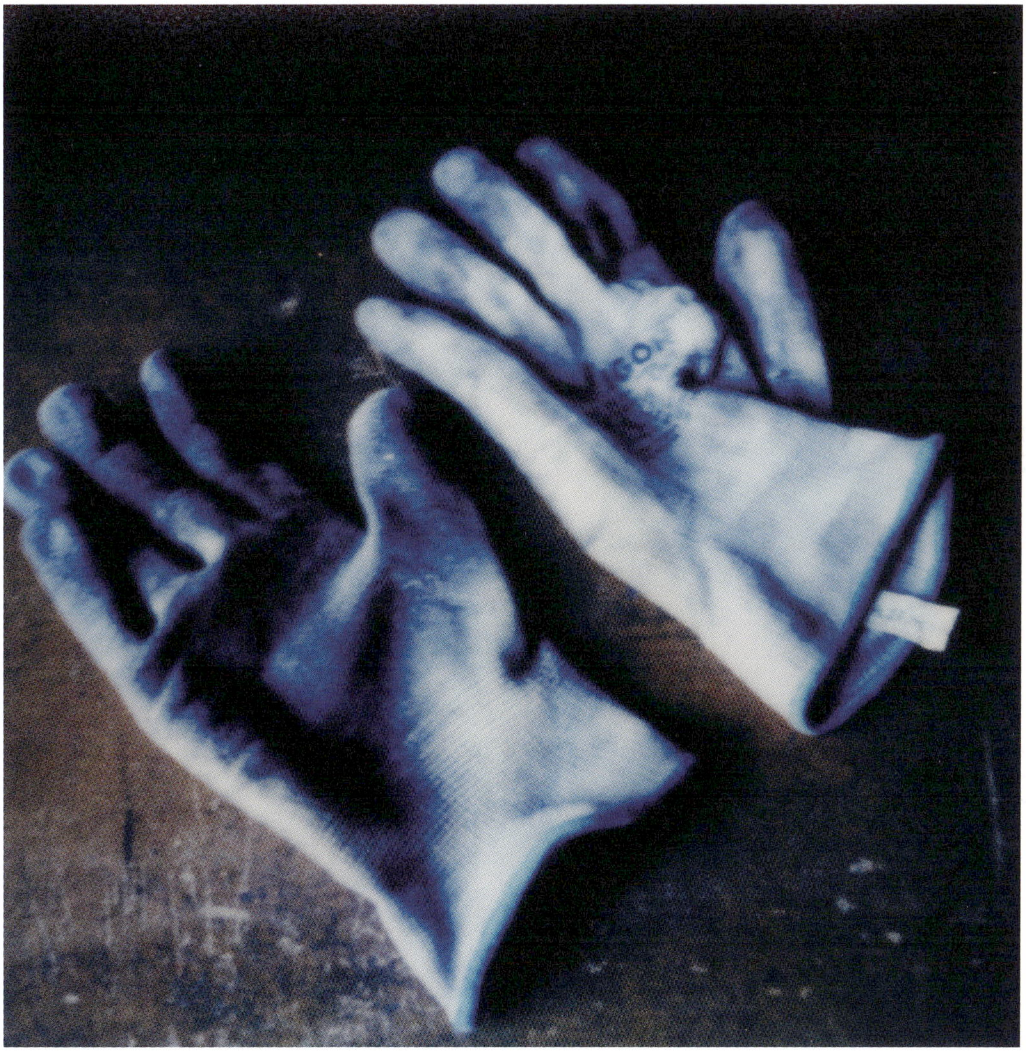

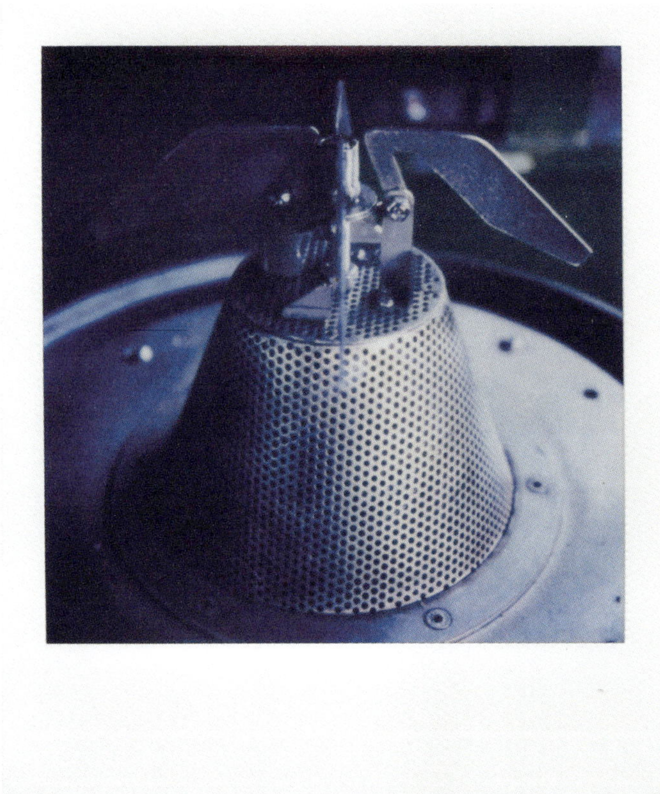

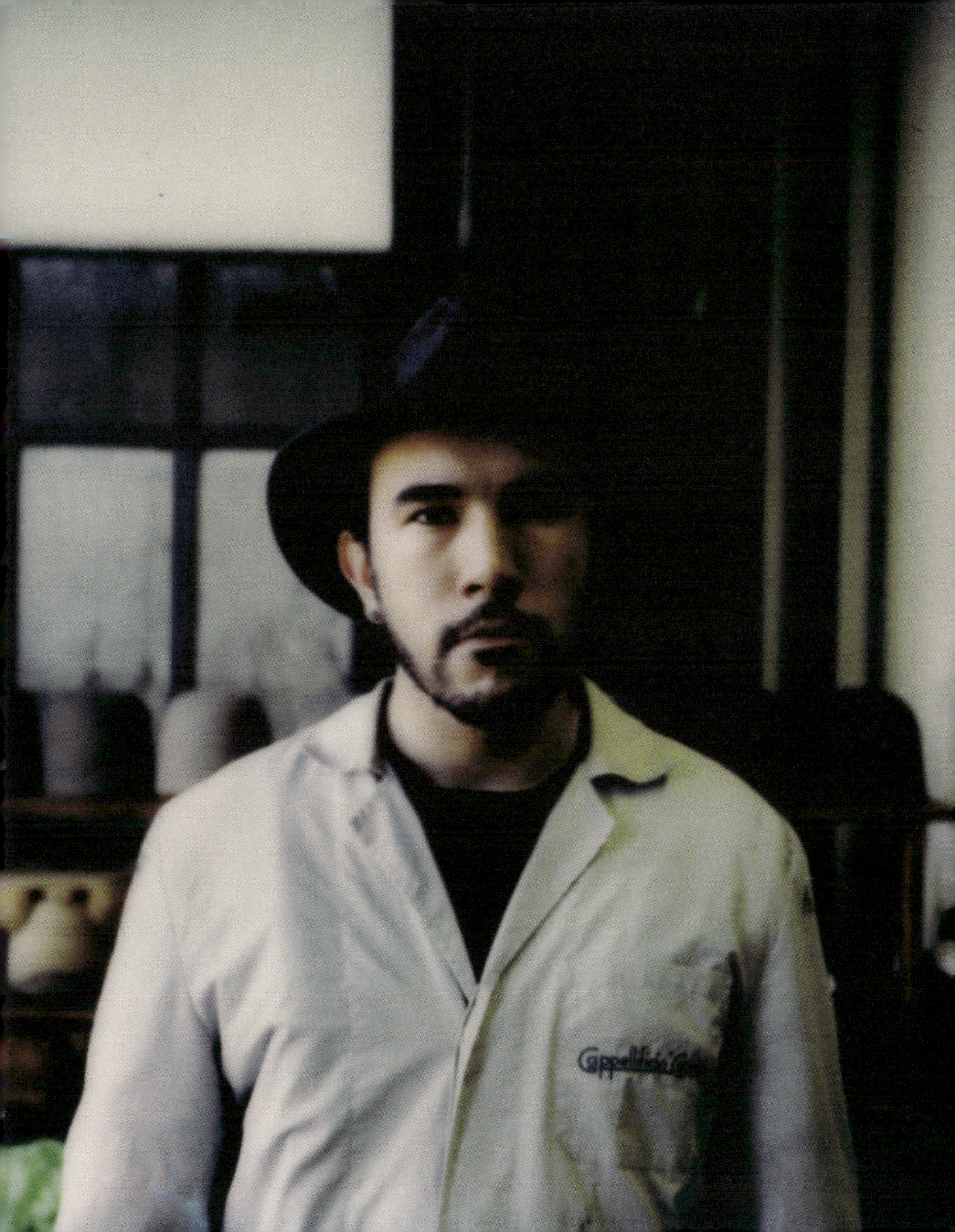

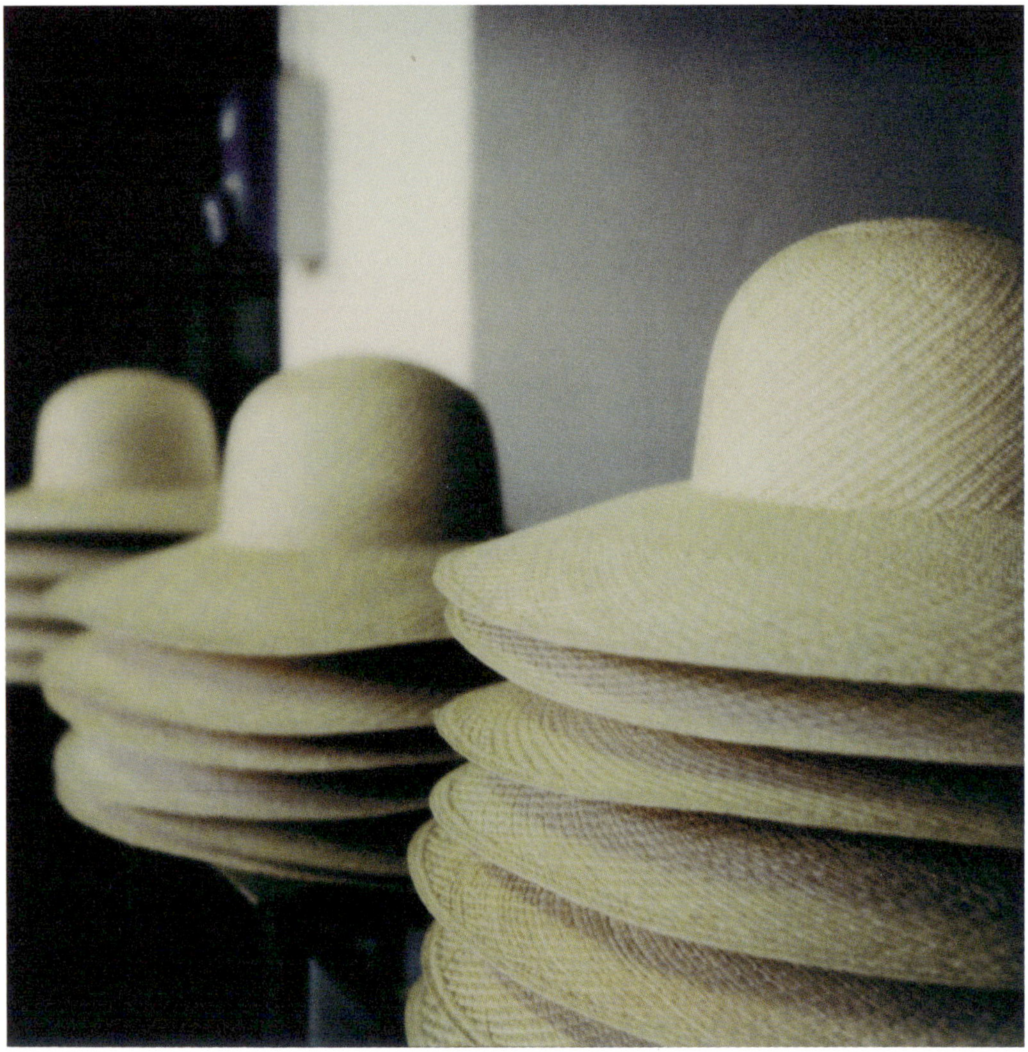

Wide brim straw hats

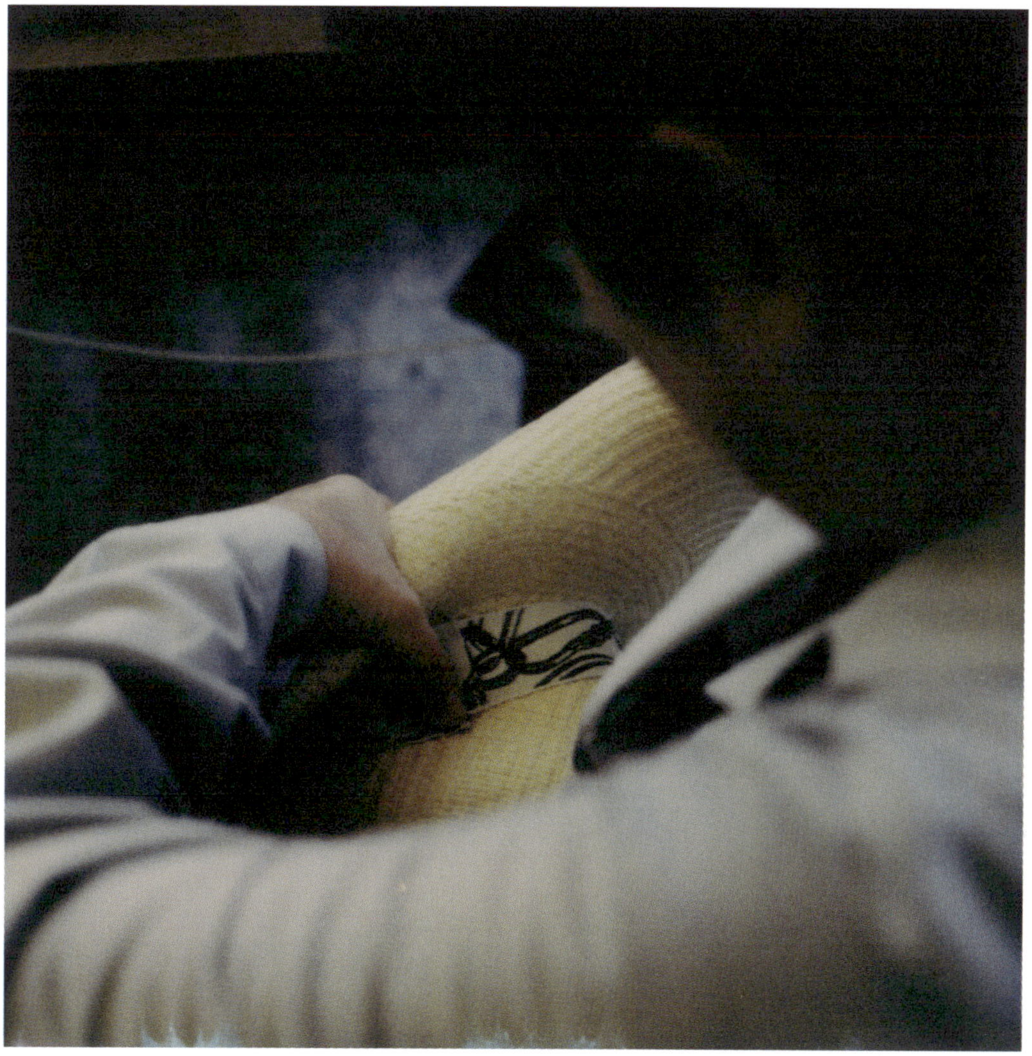

Ribbon placement

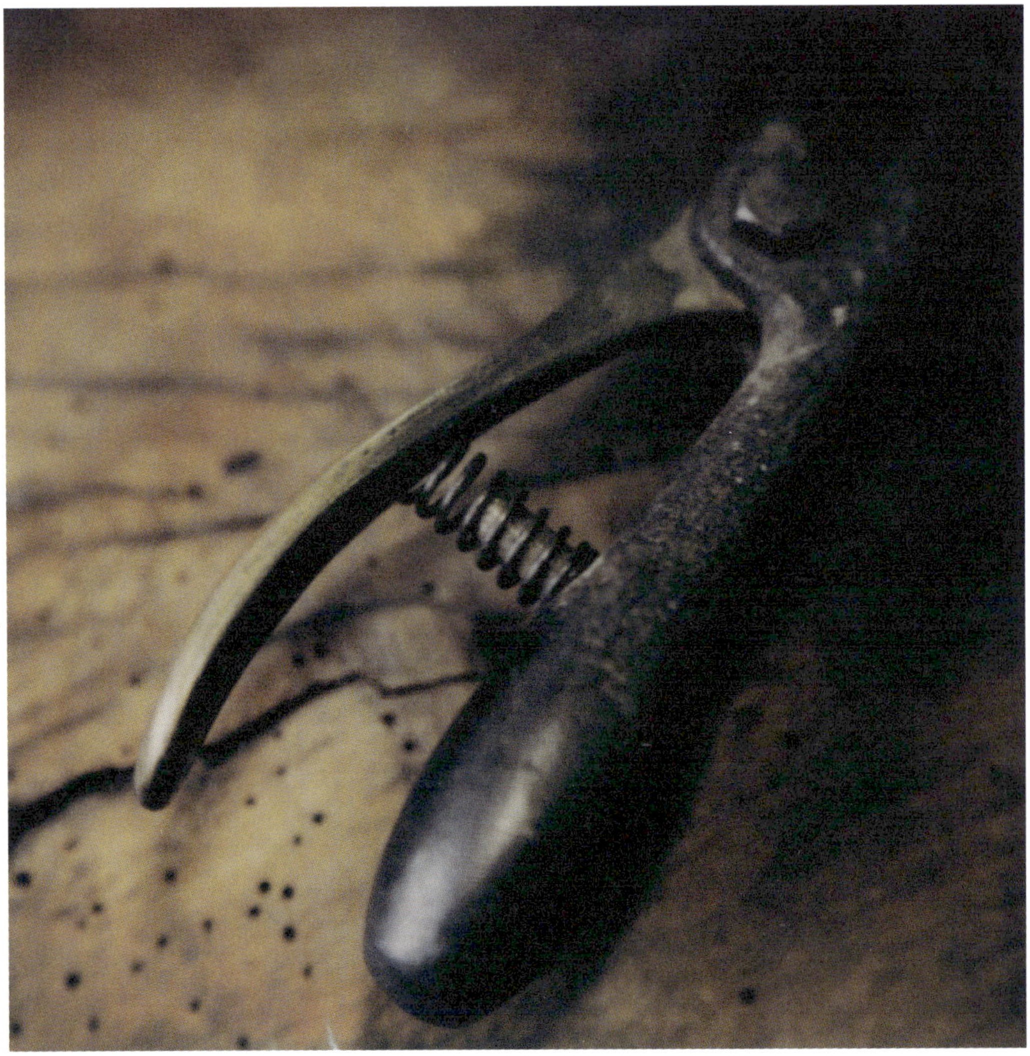

Handle of turning machine

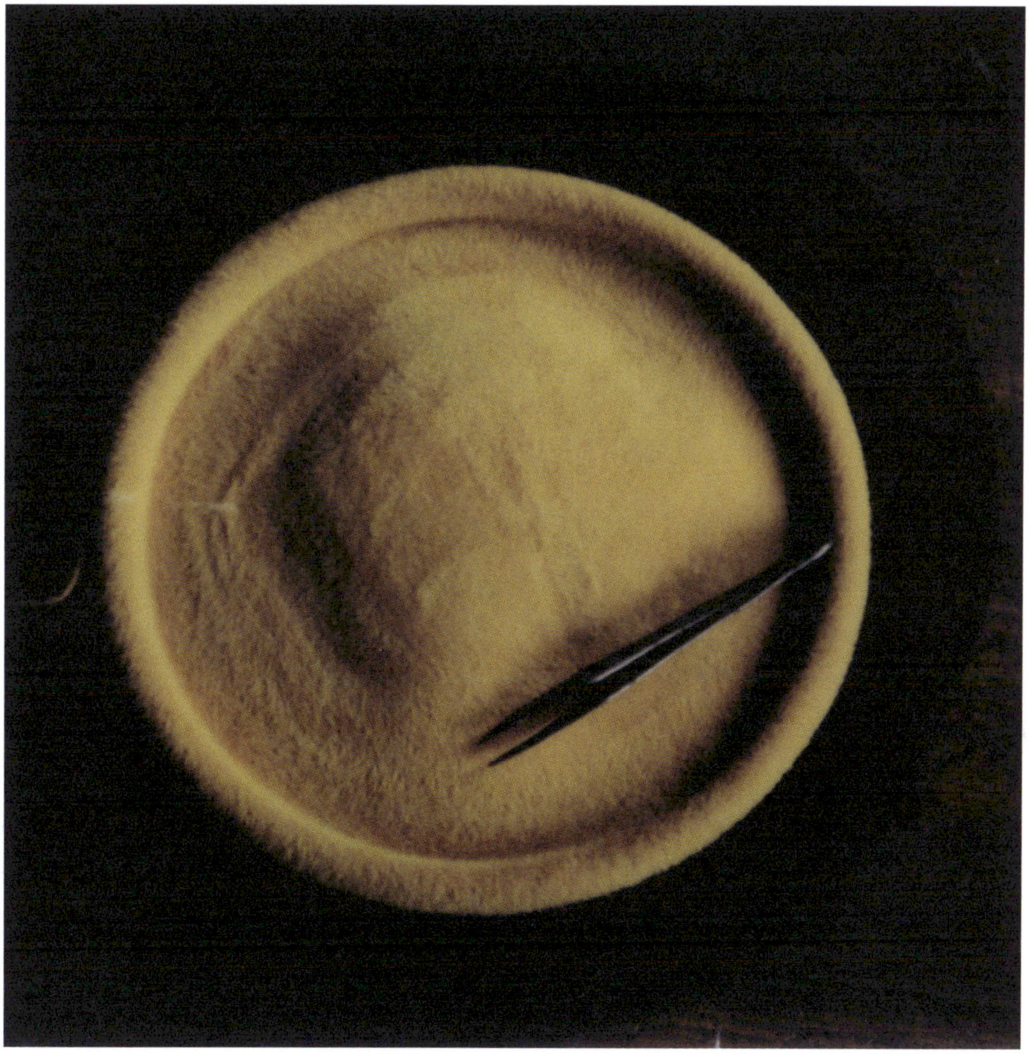

Scissors on a felt plate

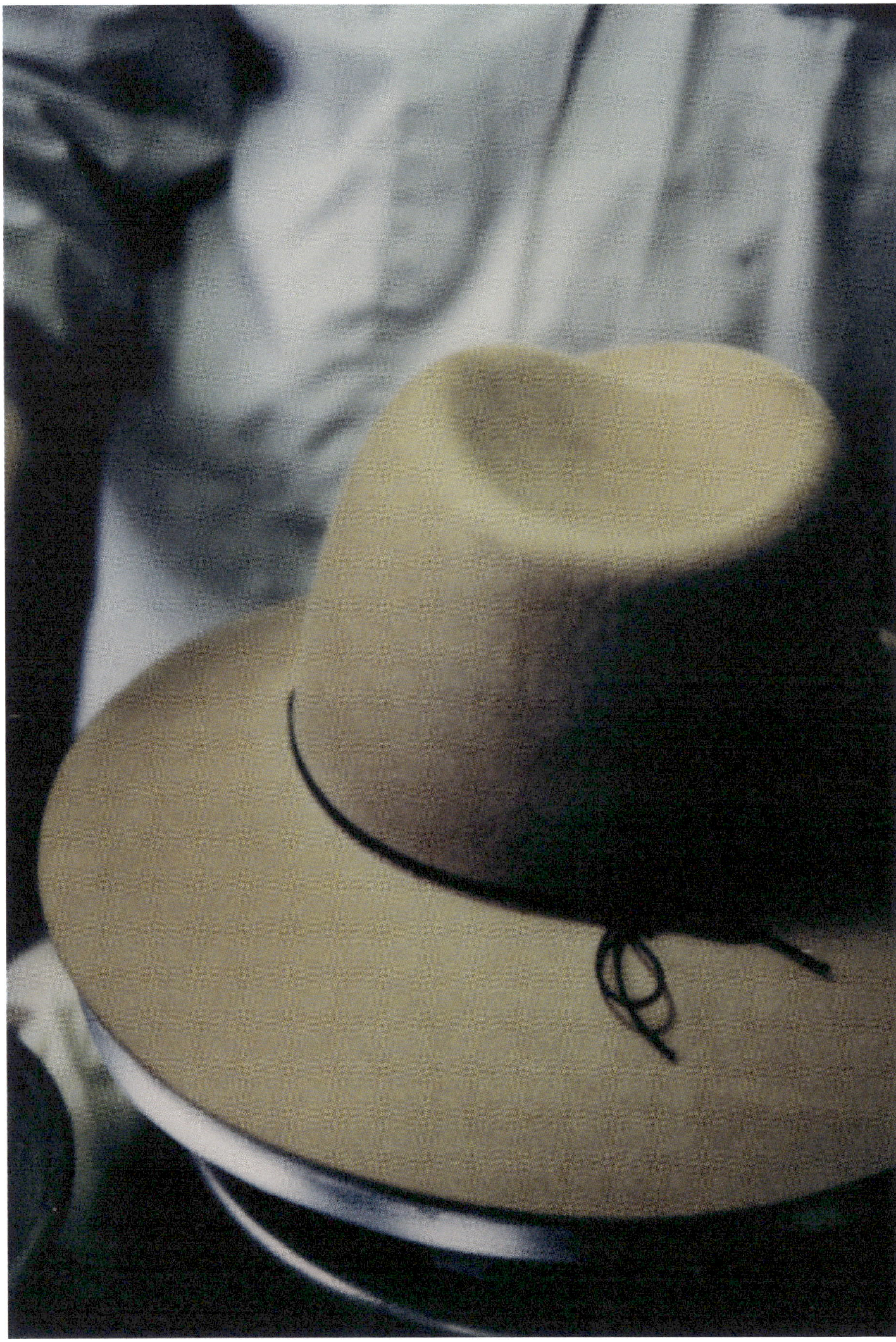

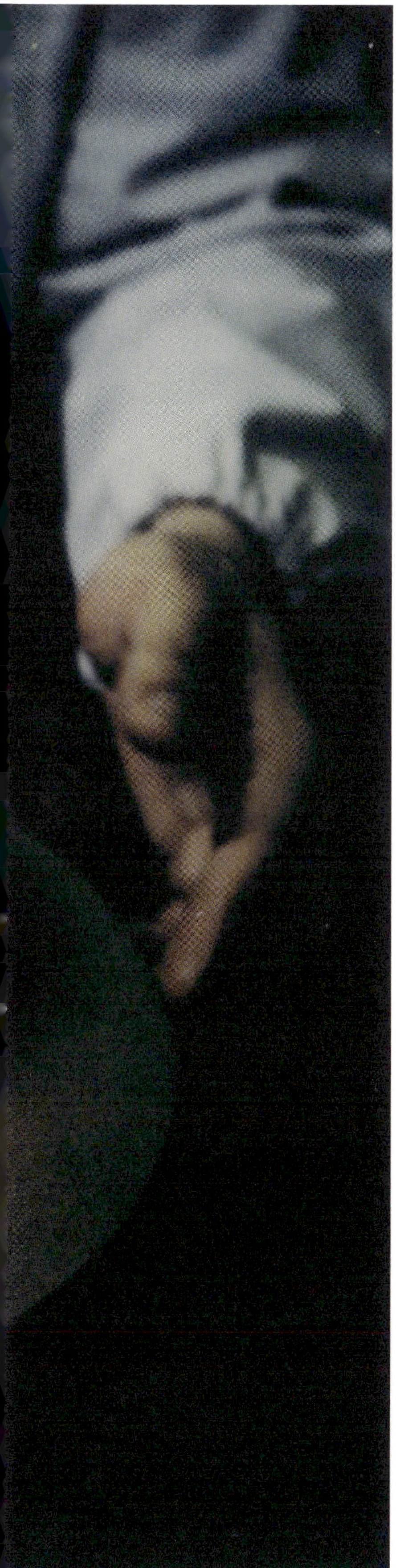

Camel colour felt hat

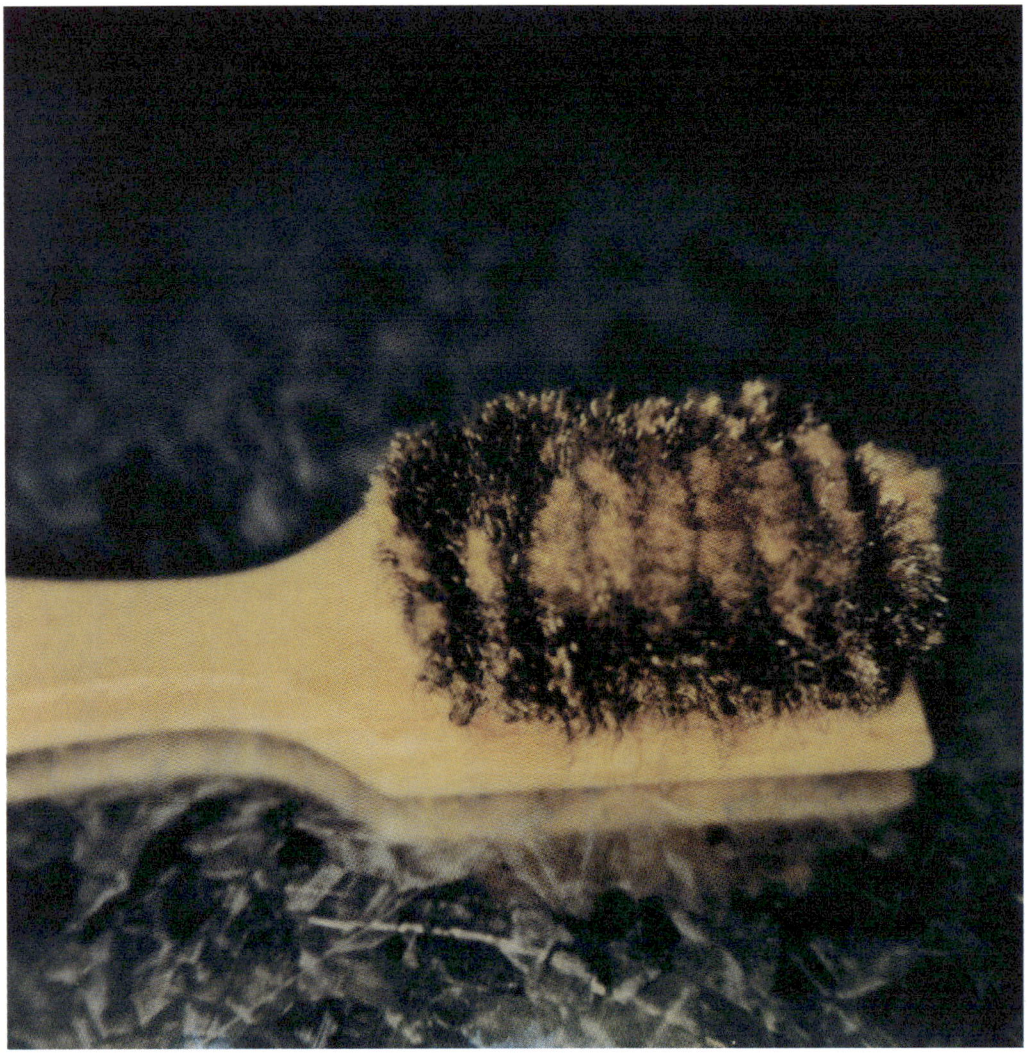

Brush with metal bristles

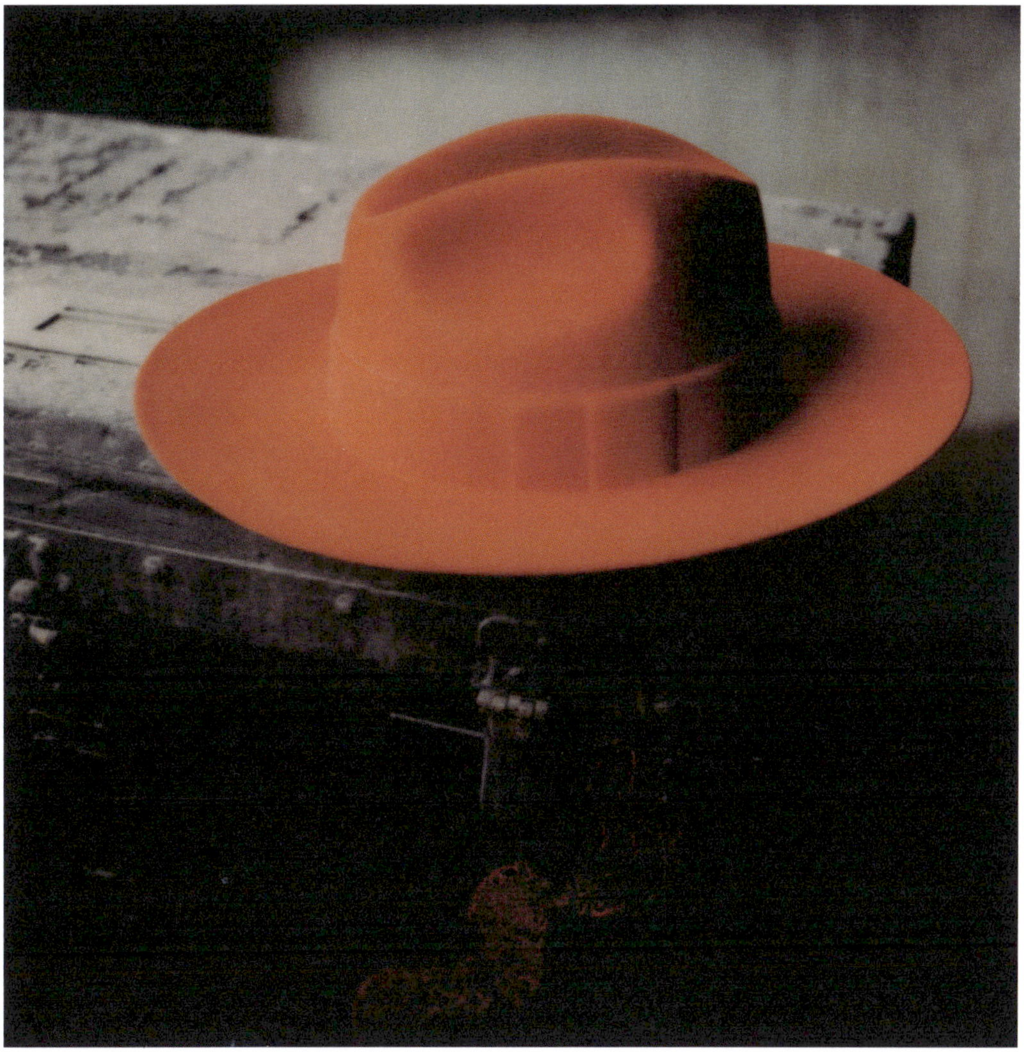

Embossed Steve hat

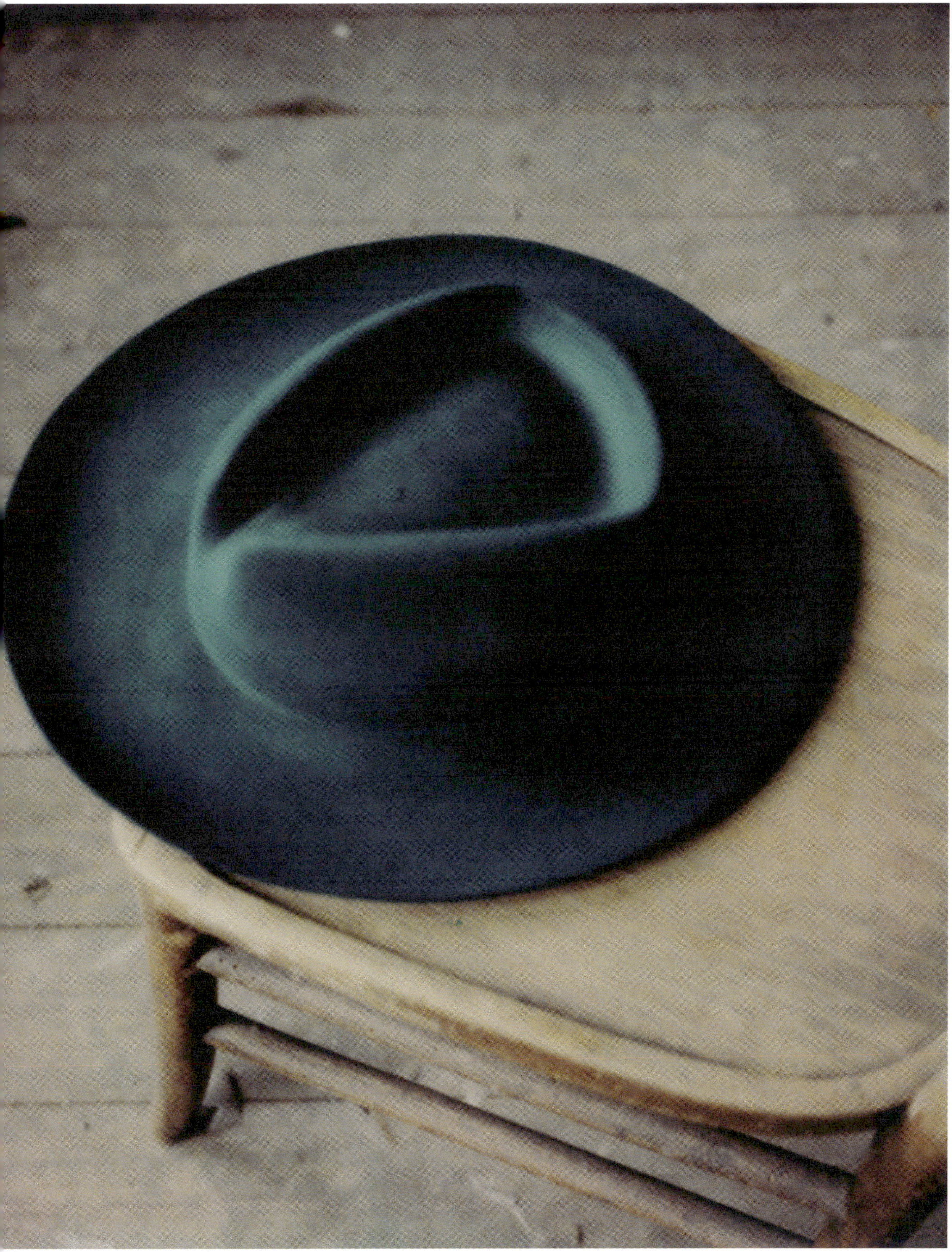

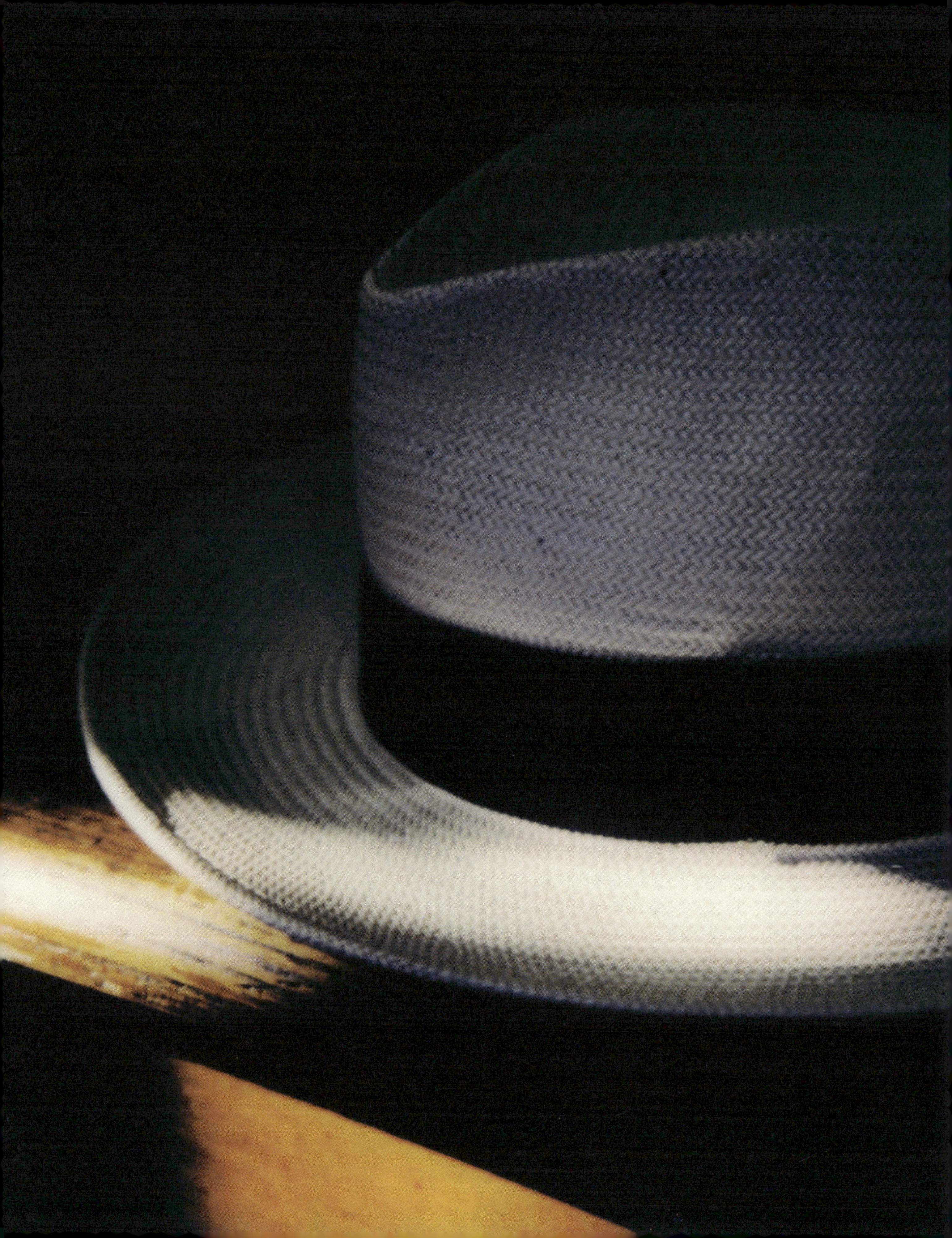

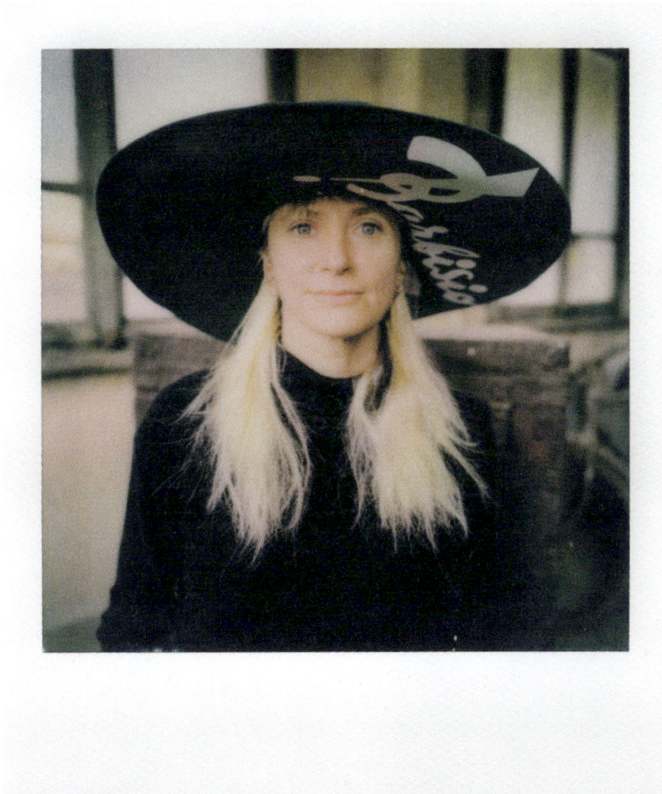

White paper hat

V.B., with green Paloma Barbisio

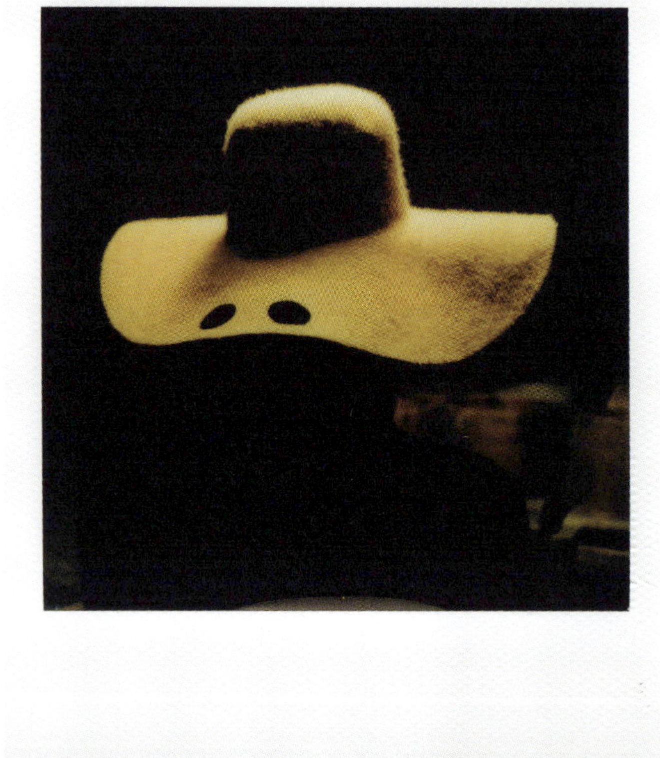

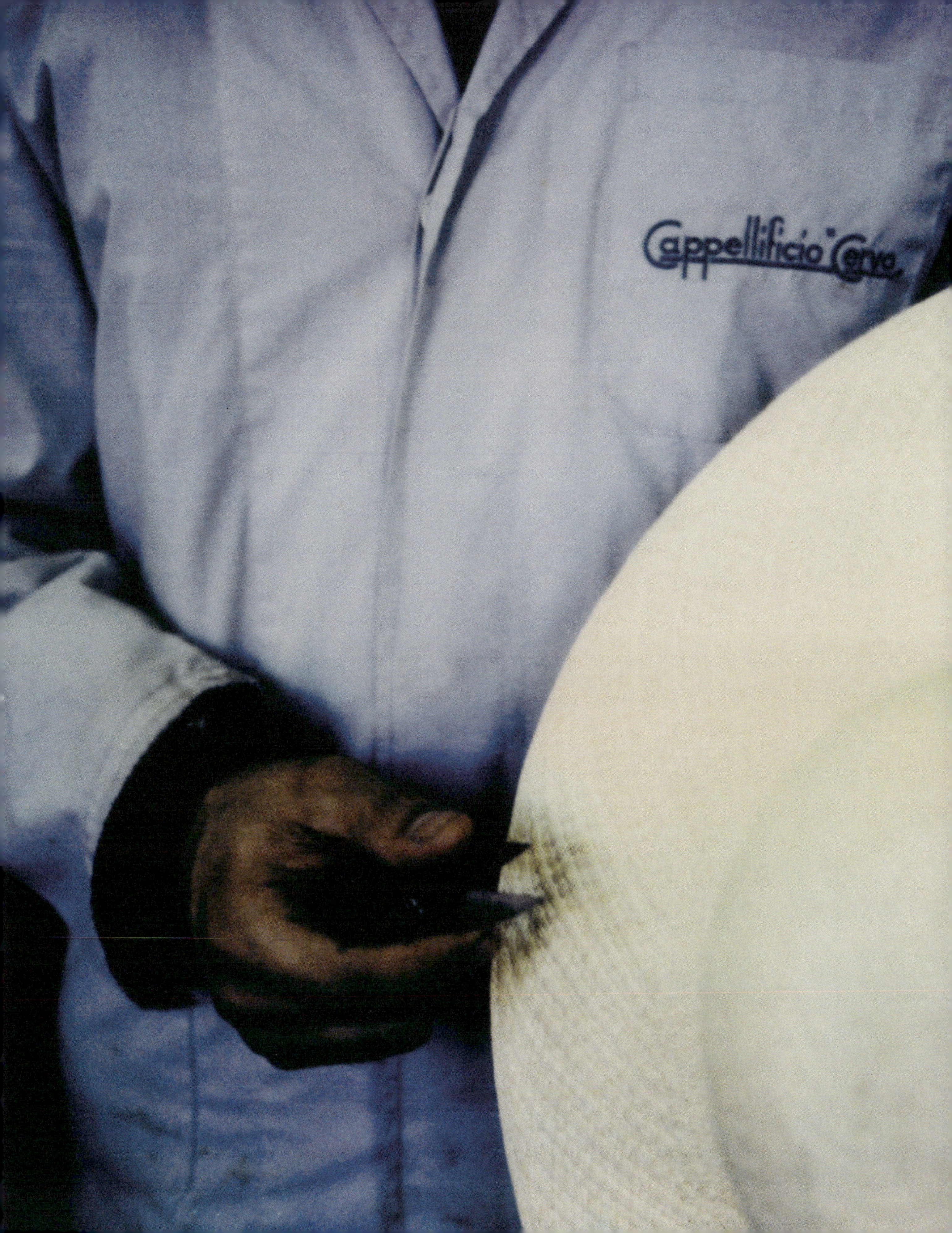
Cappellificio "Cervo"

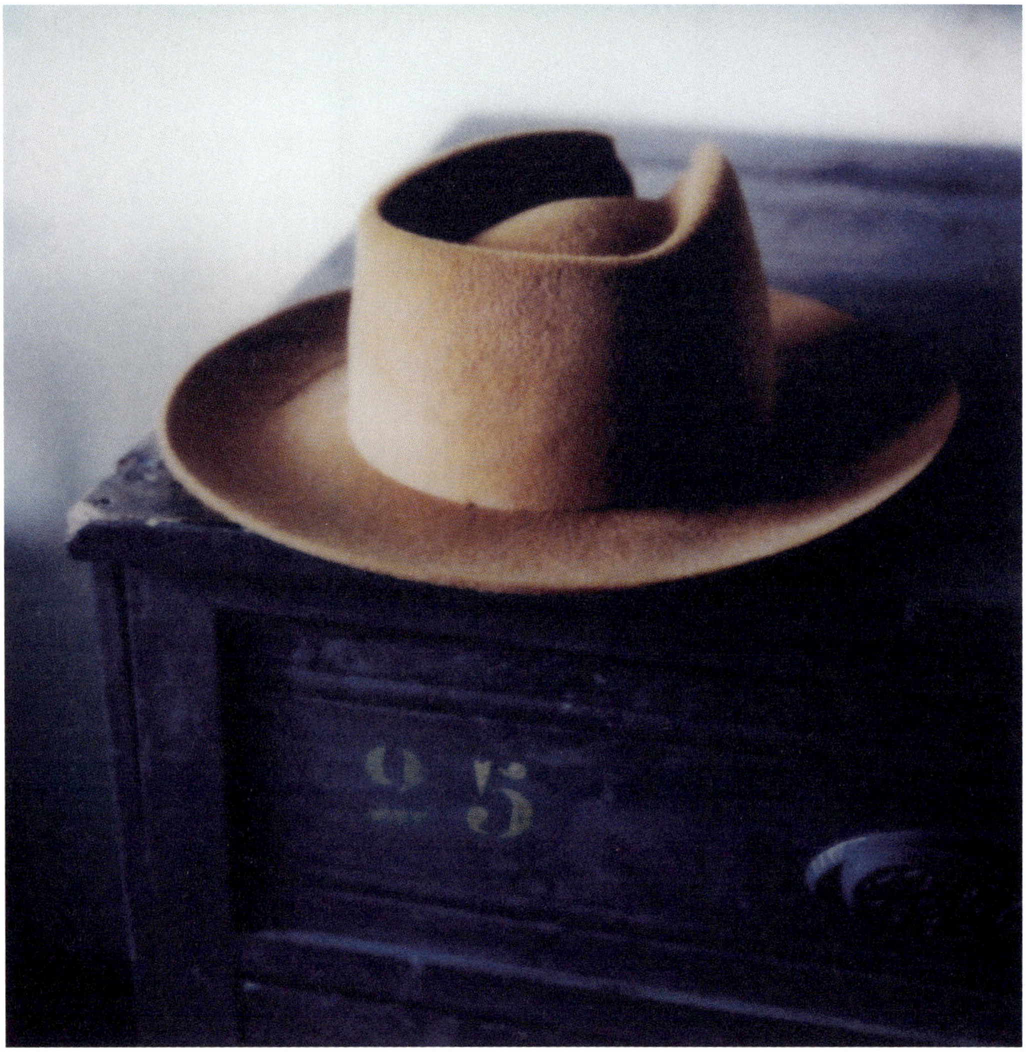

Marcello n. 25

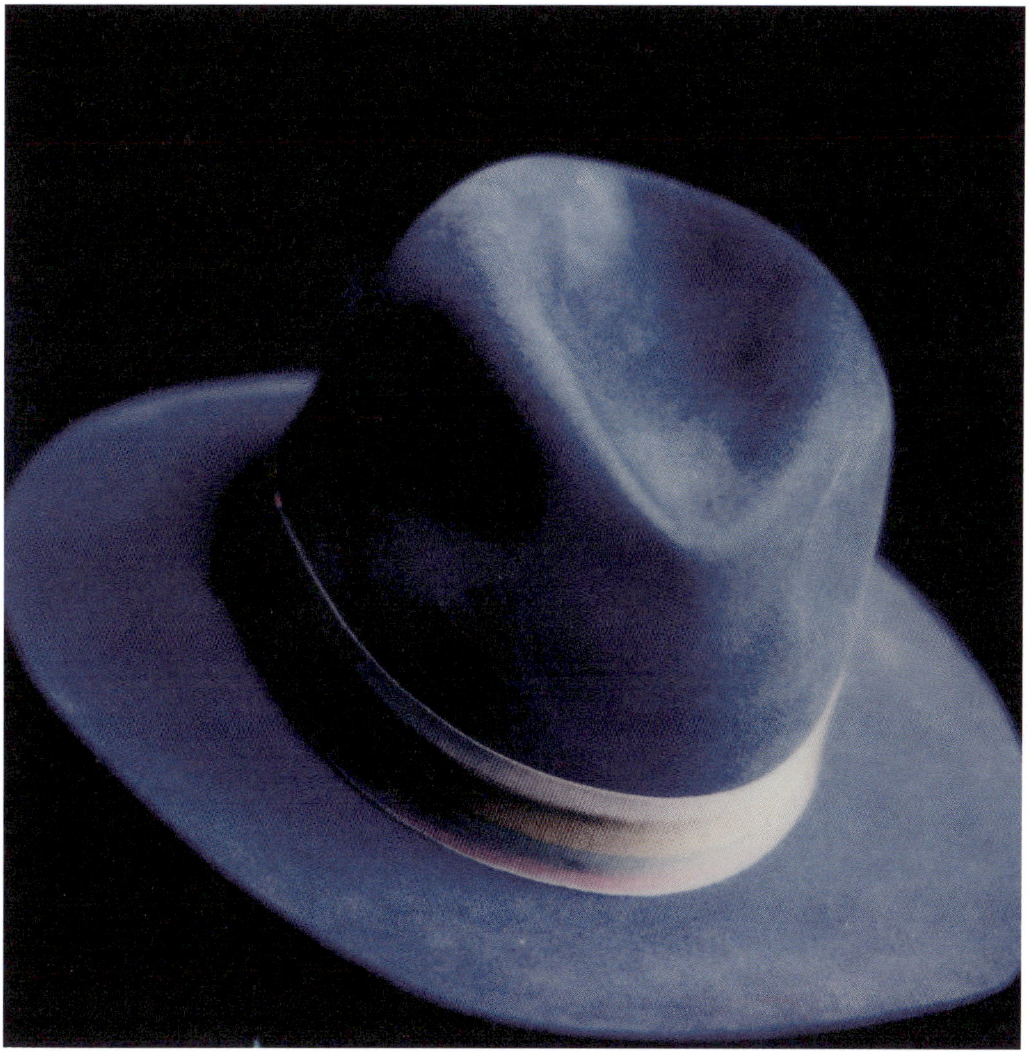

Fedora formed by hand

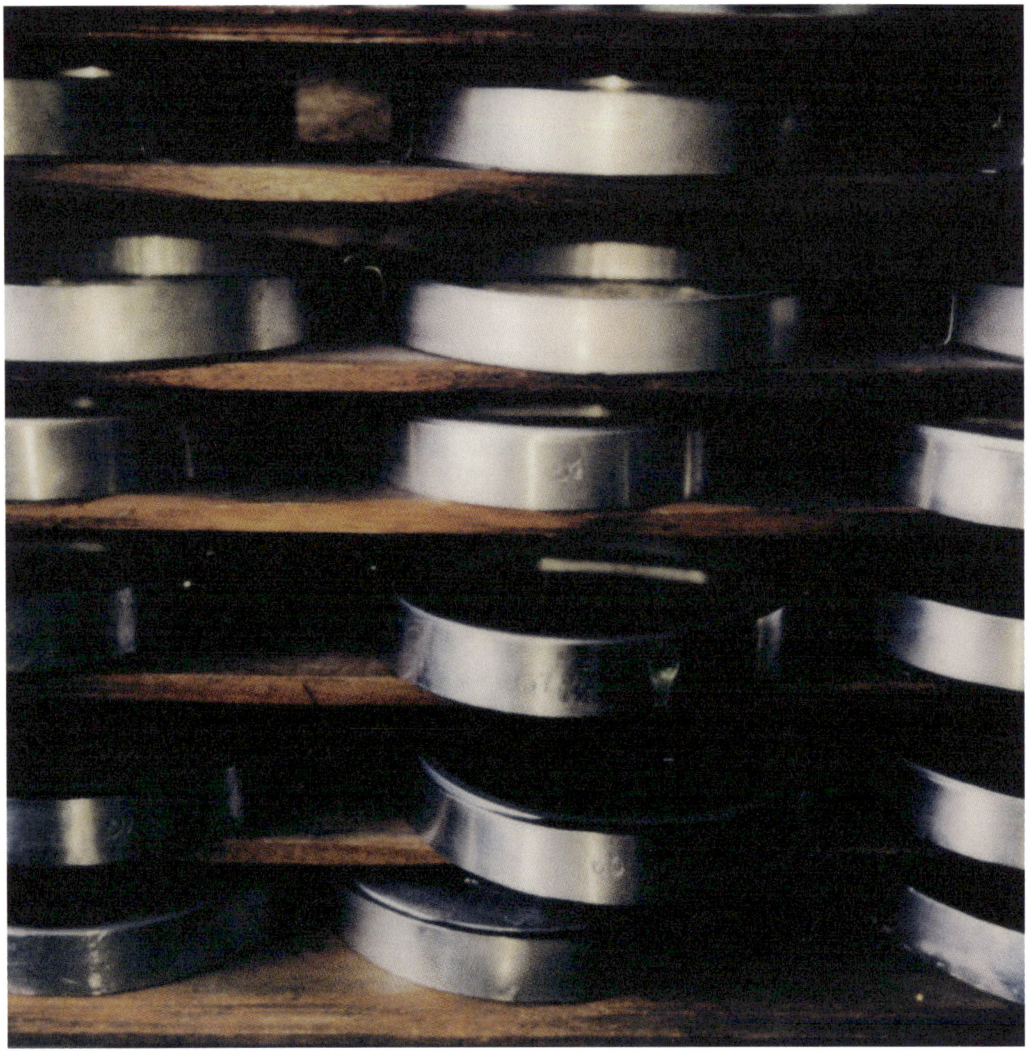

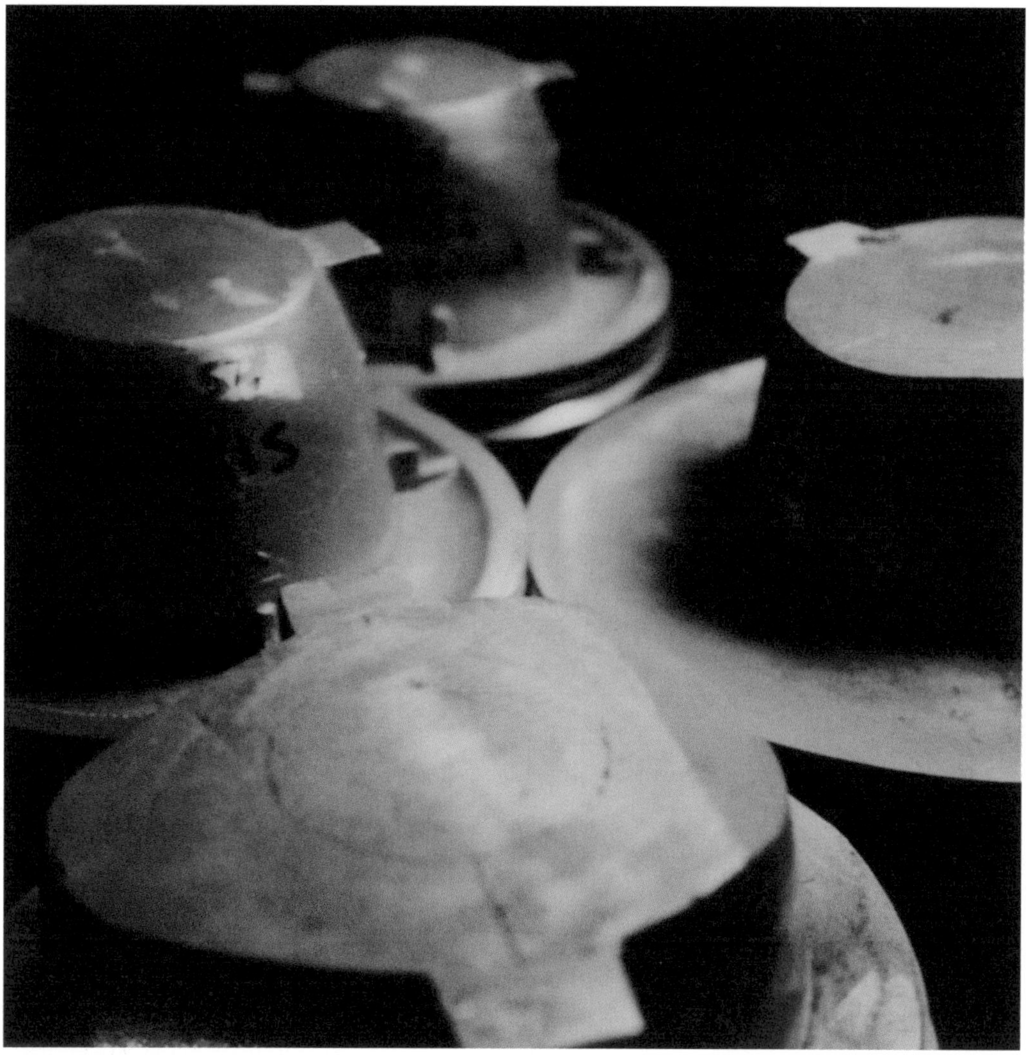

Aluminium hat blocks

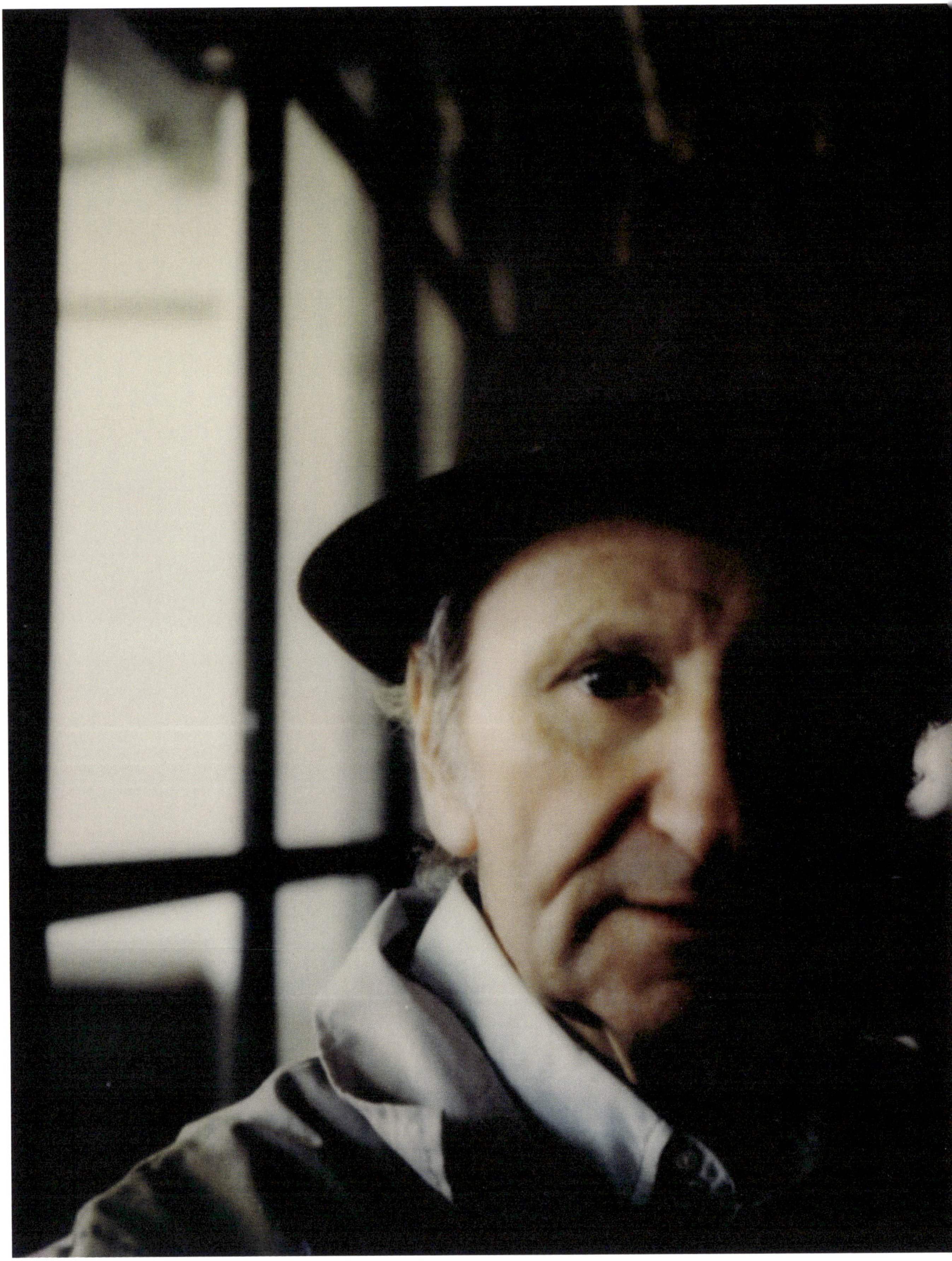

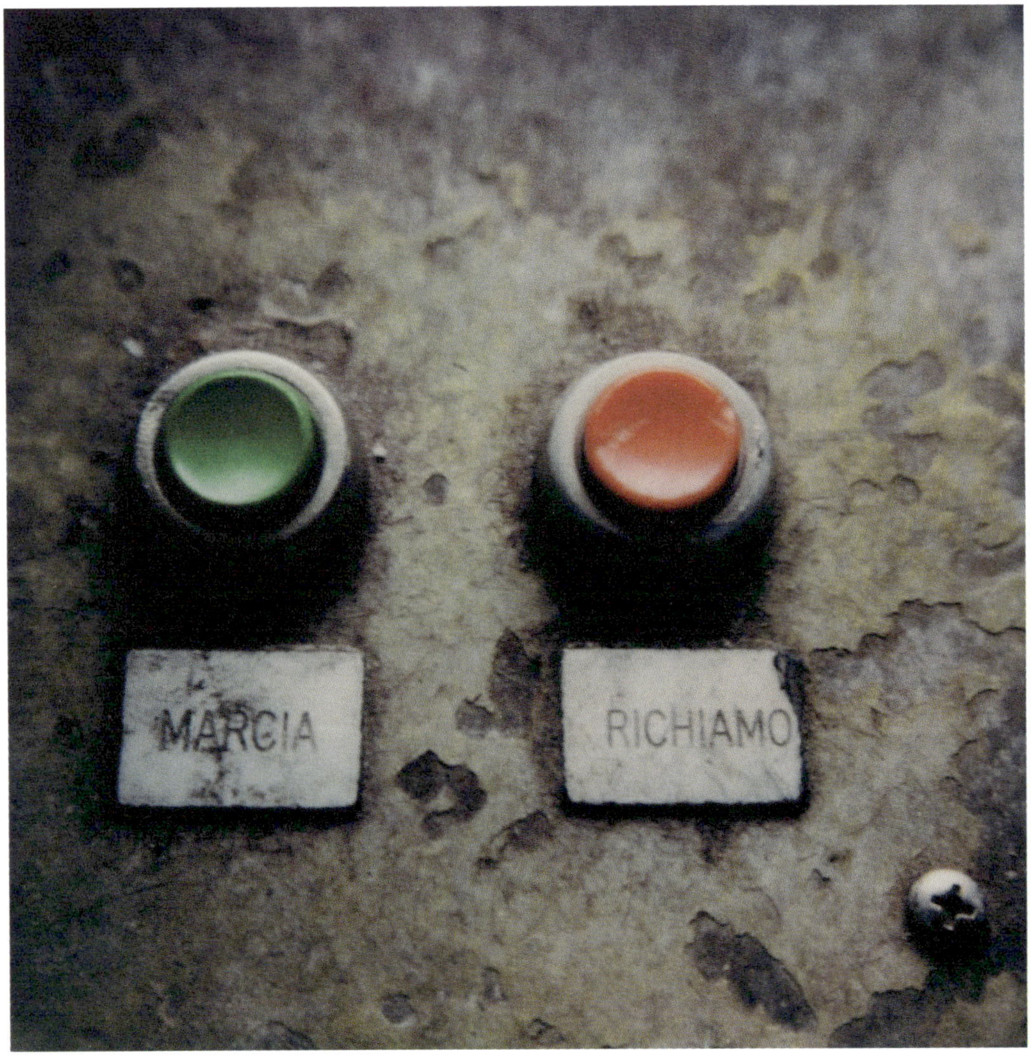

Start and reverse push button of hat block machine

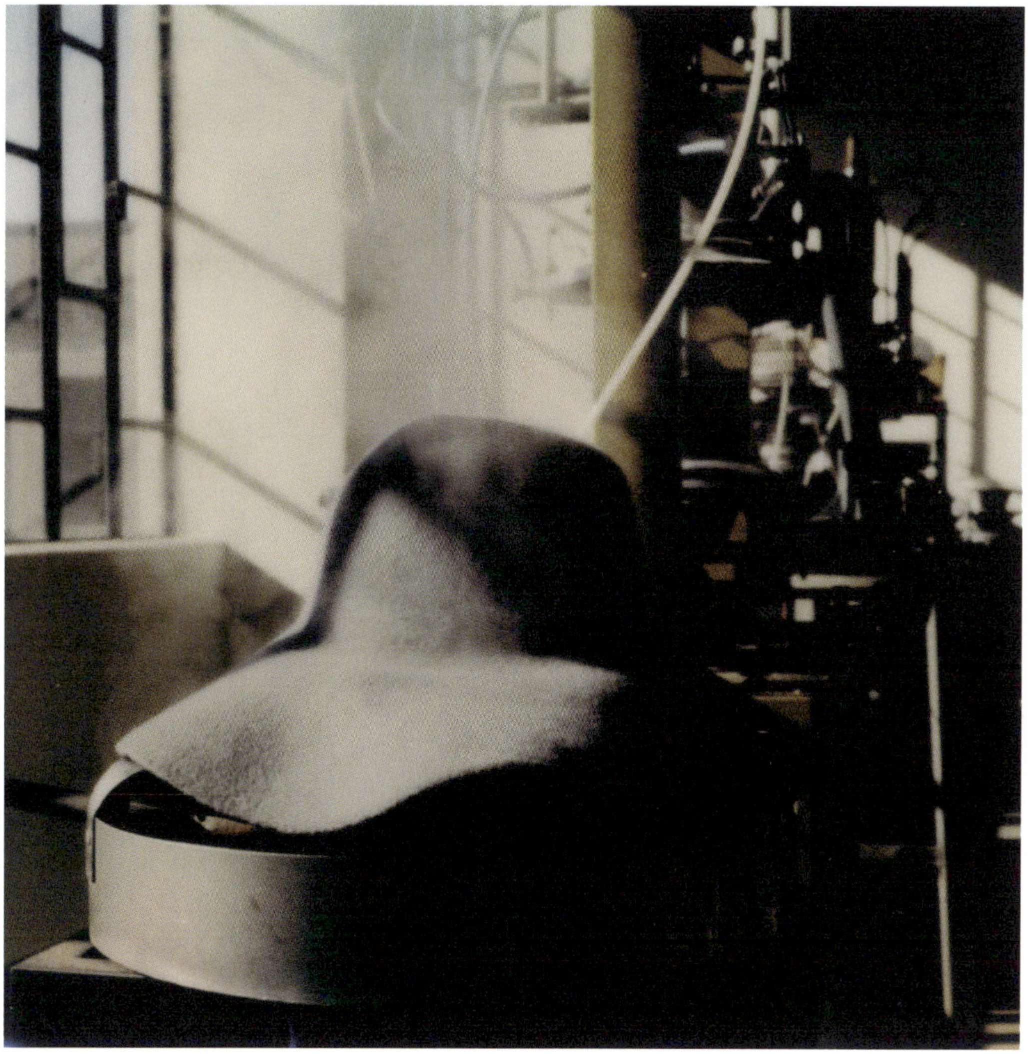

Felt cone on the steam

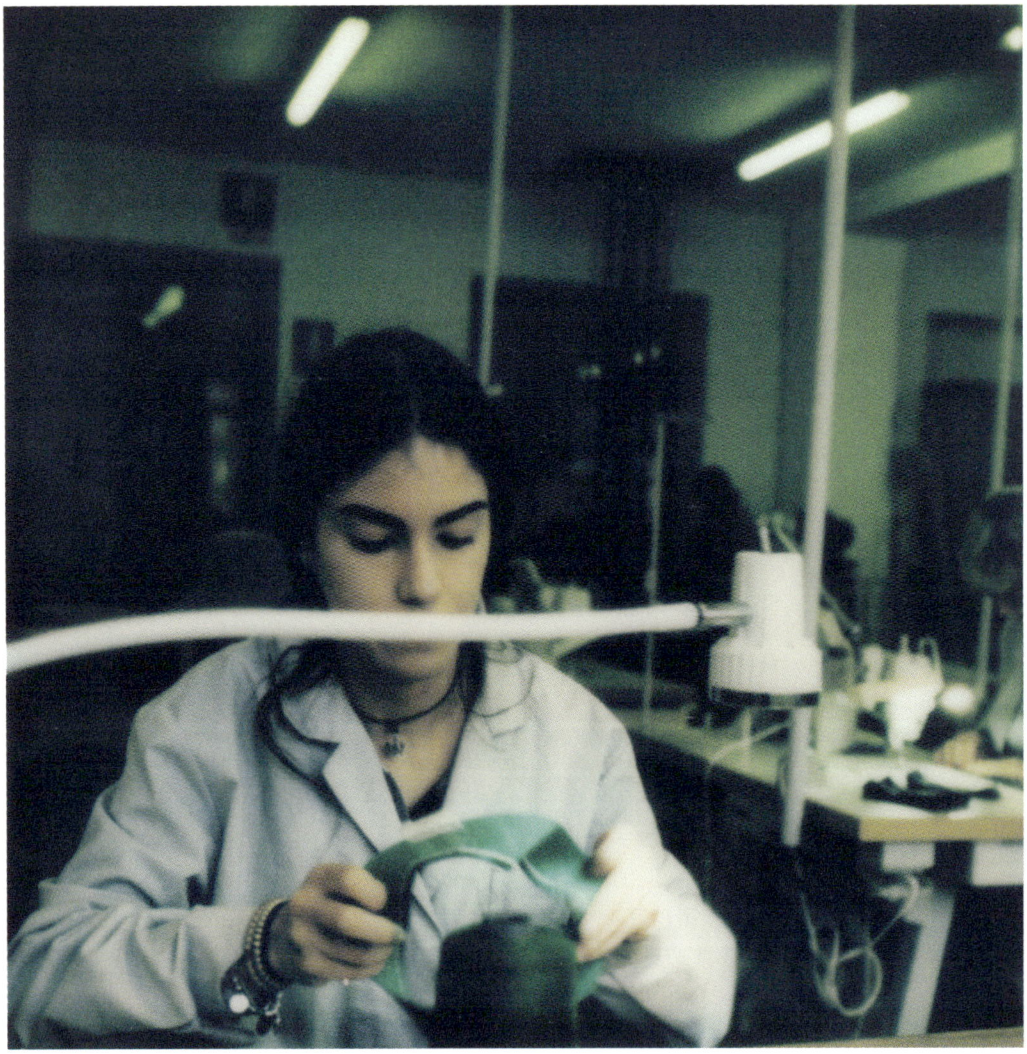

Hat trimming laboratory

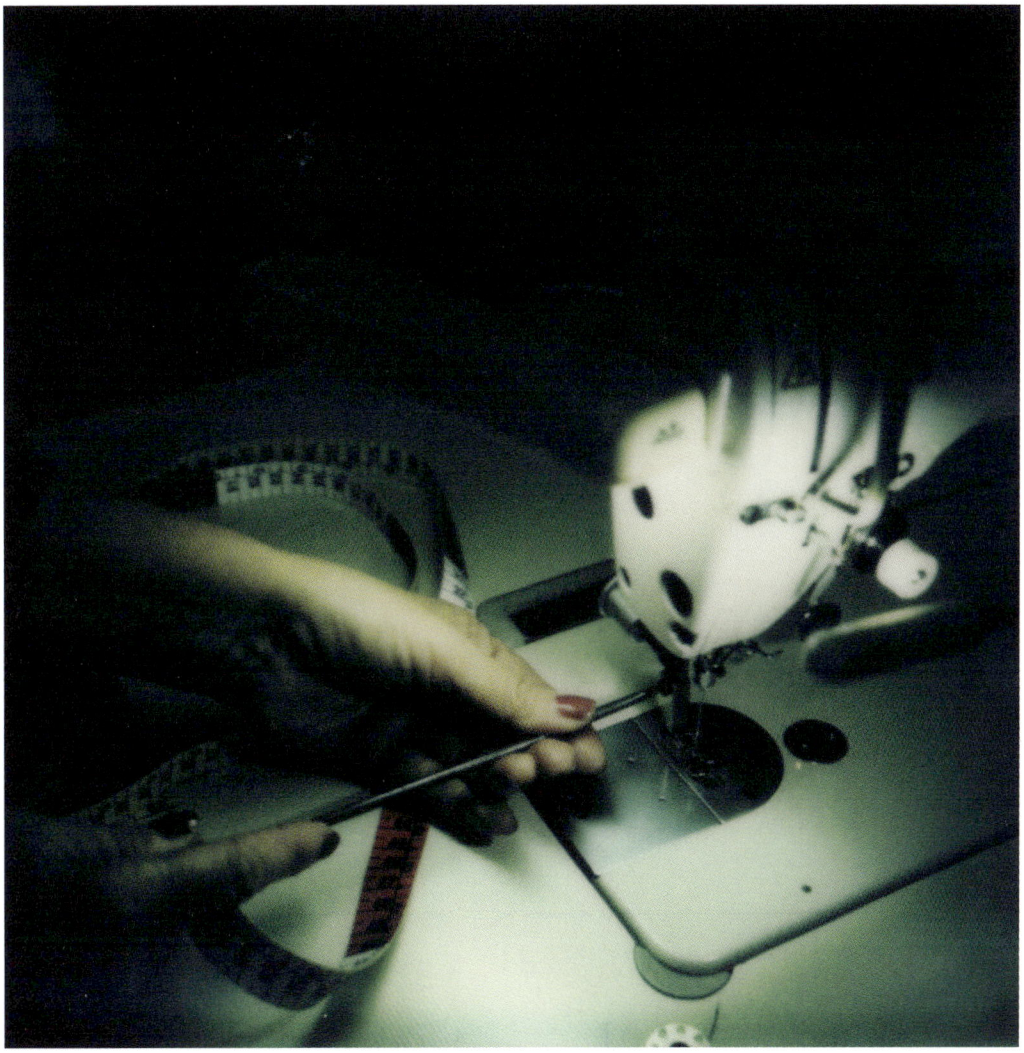

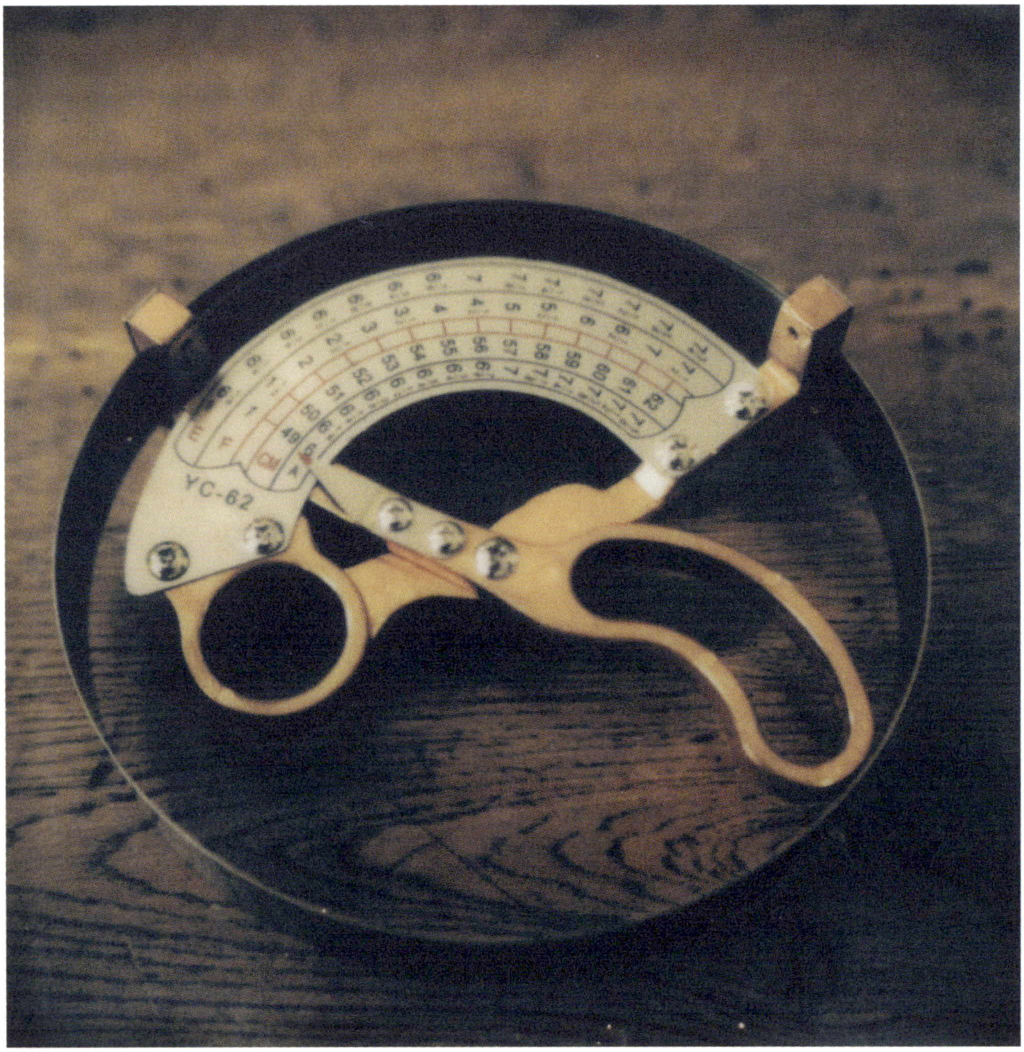

Hat circumference measuring instrument

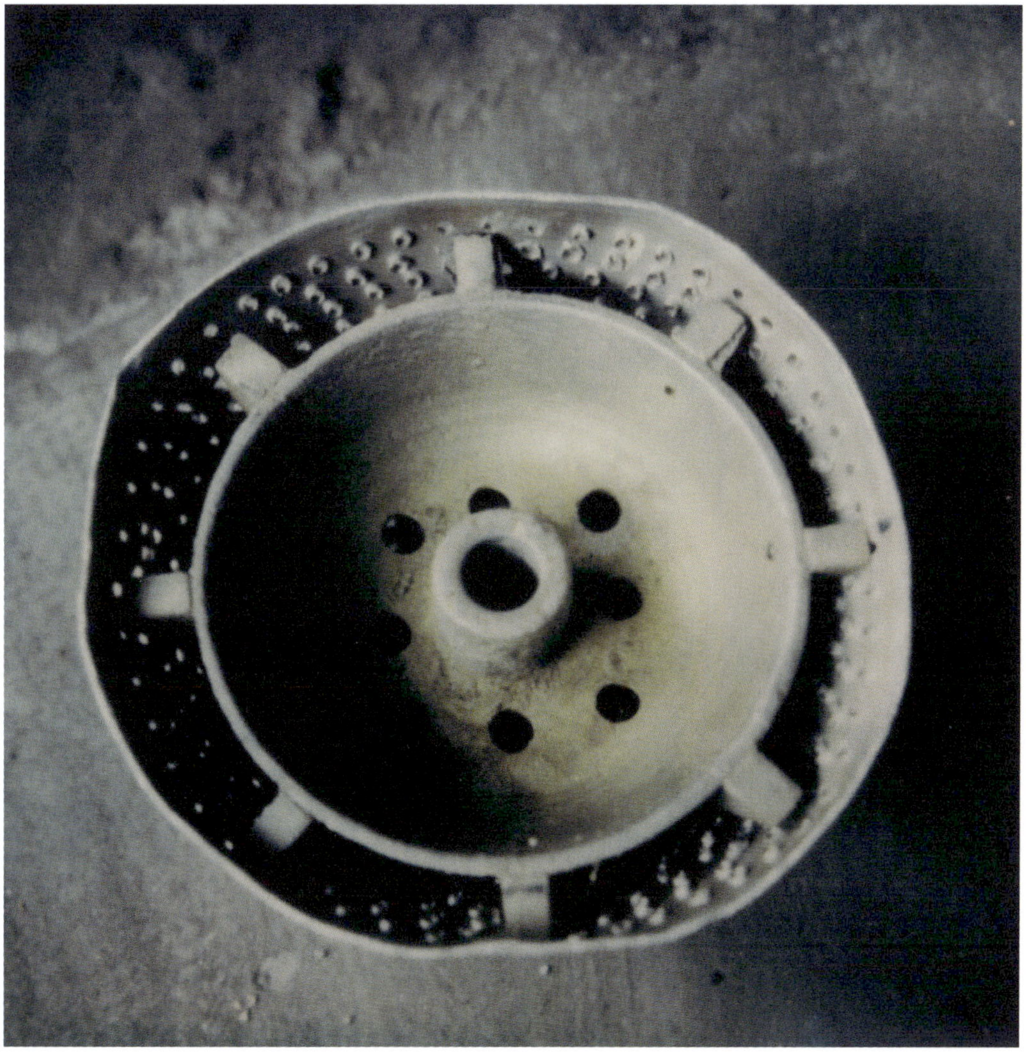

Aluminium cone

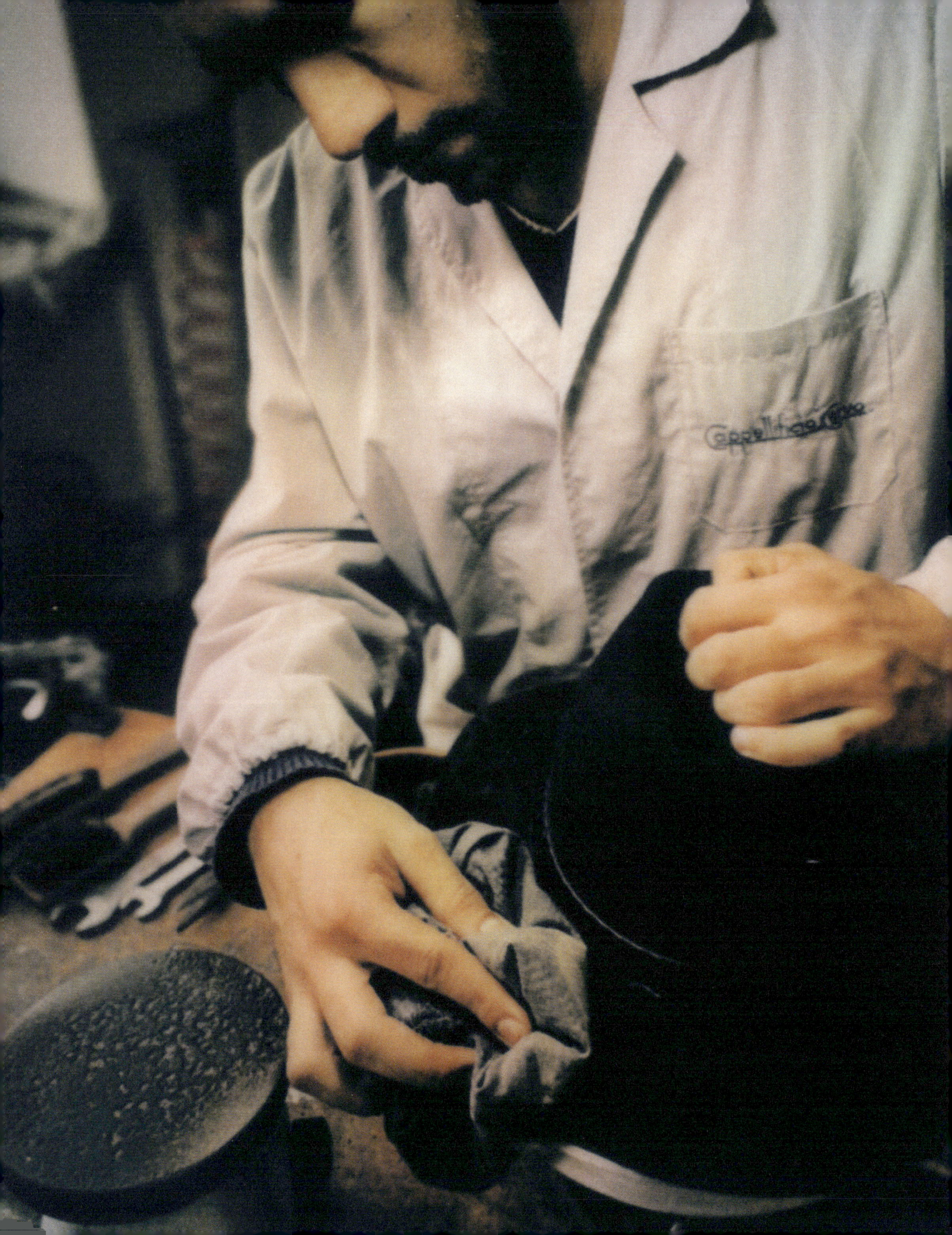

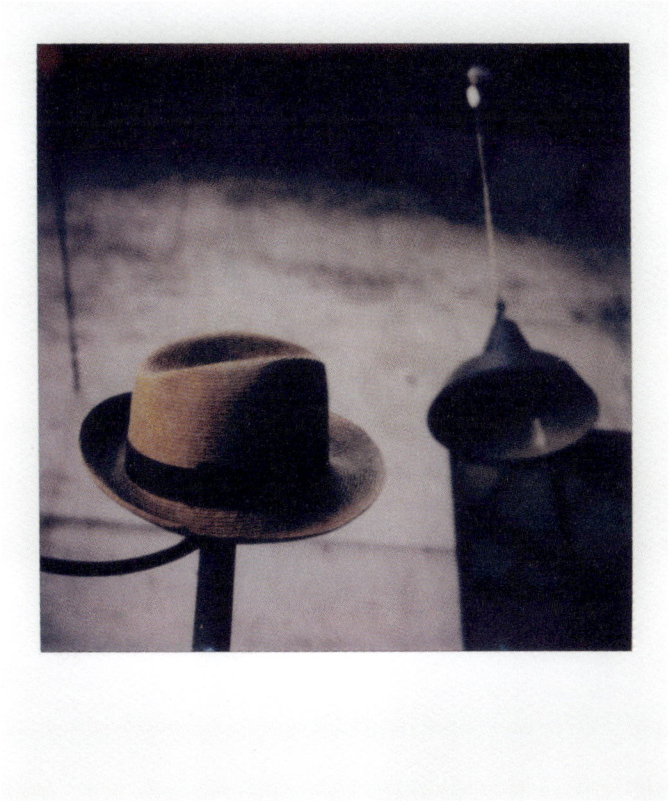

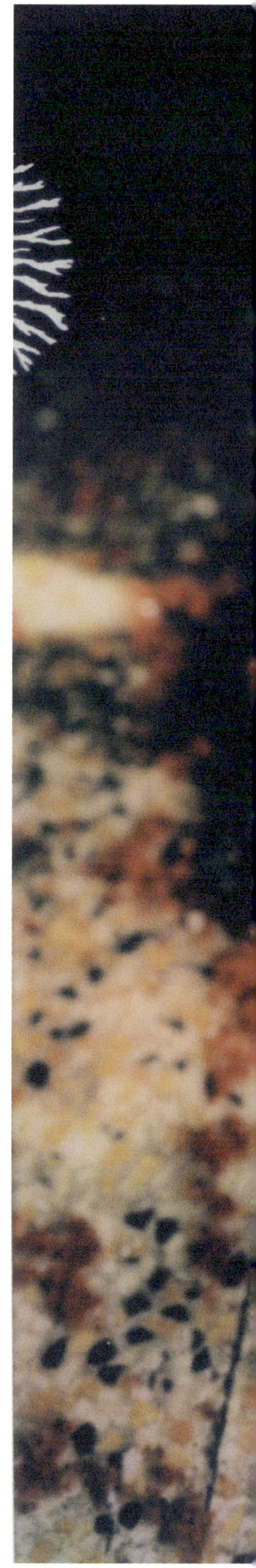

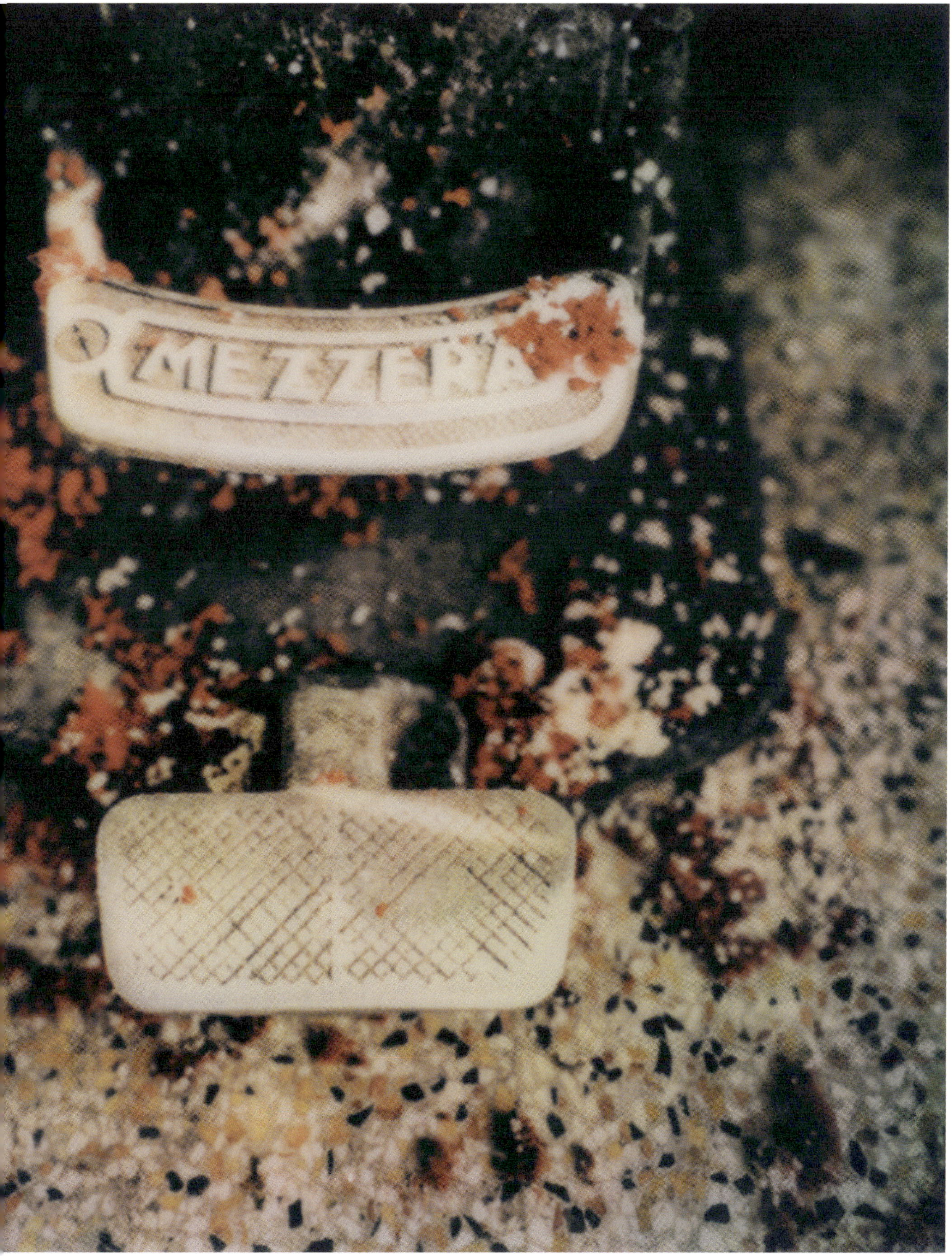
MEZZERA

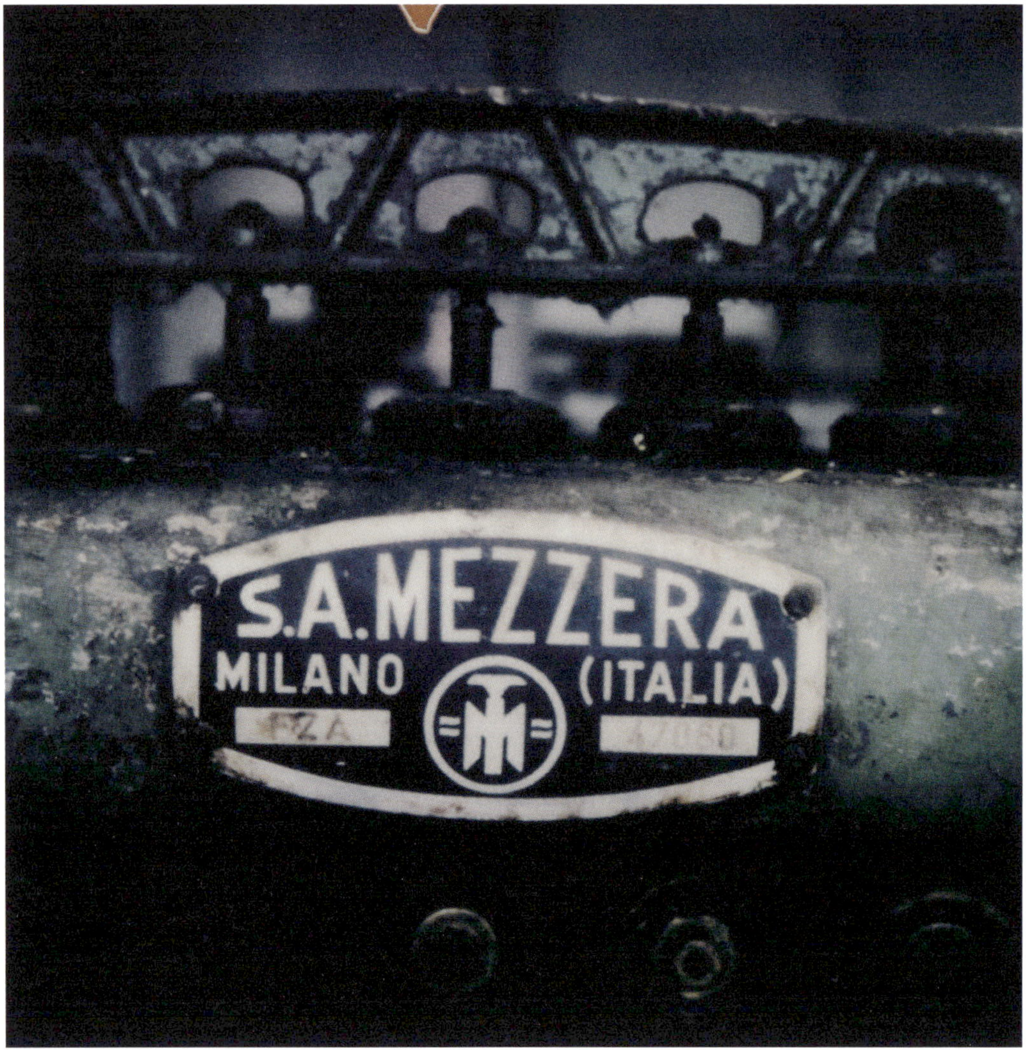

Mezzera machine

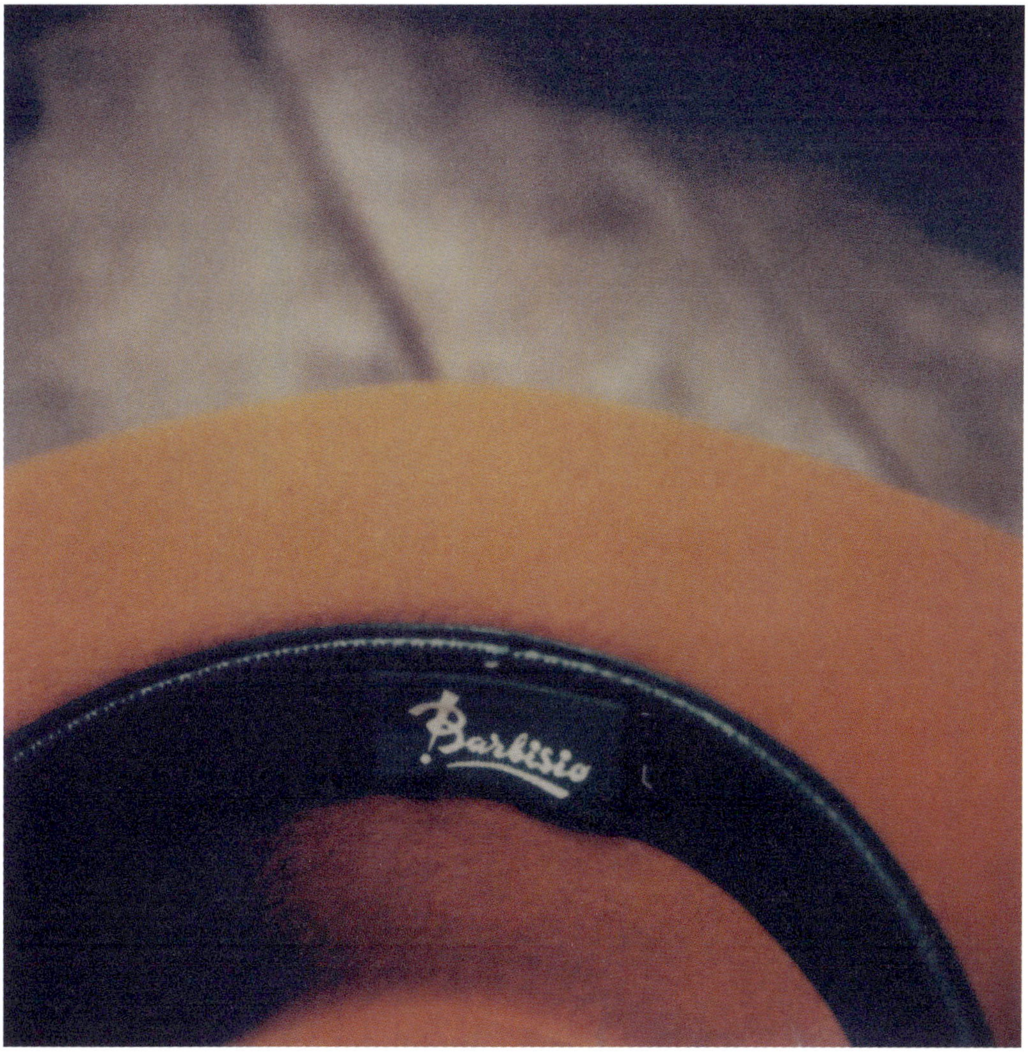

Barbisio label

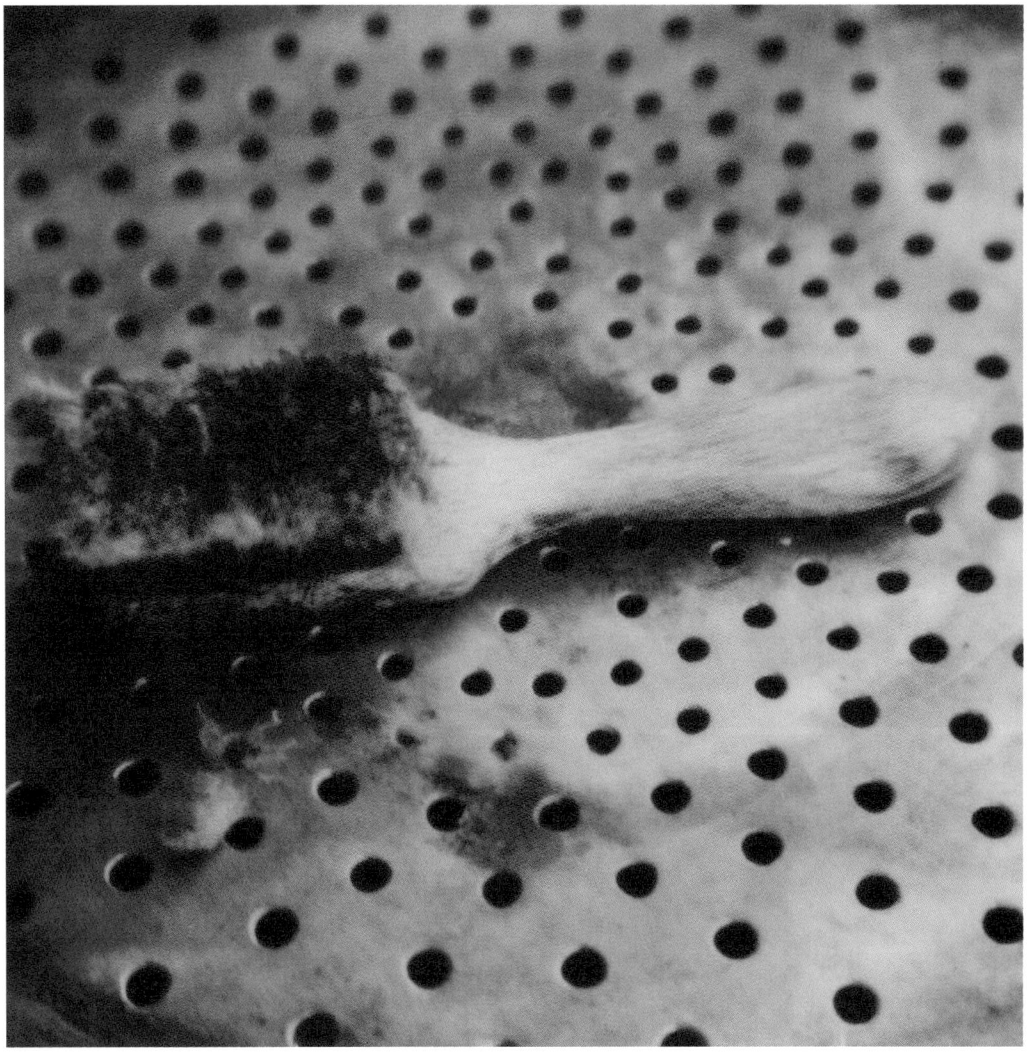

Light hair brush

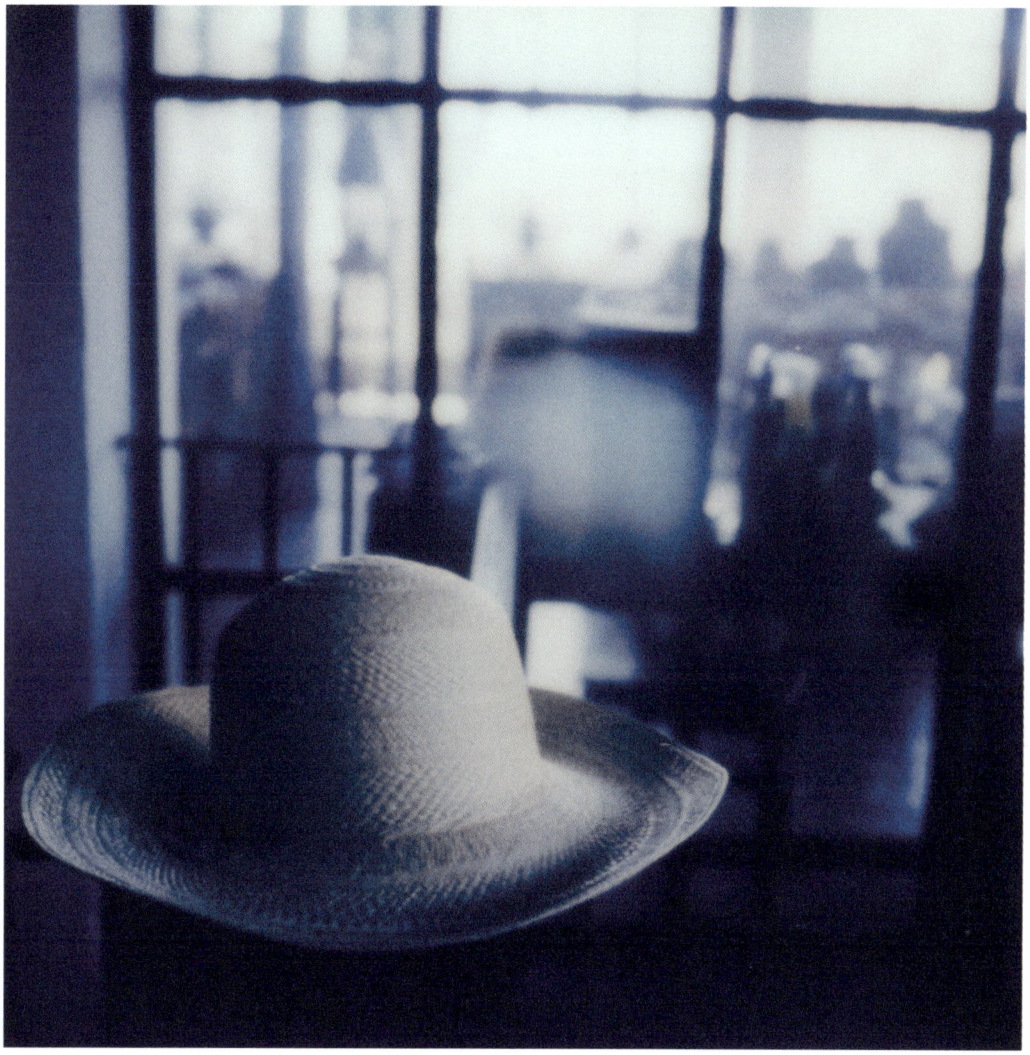

Straw capelina

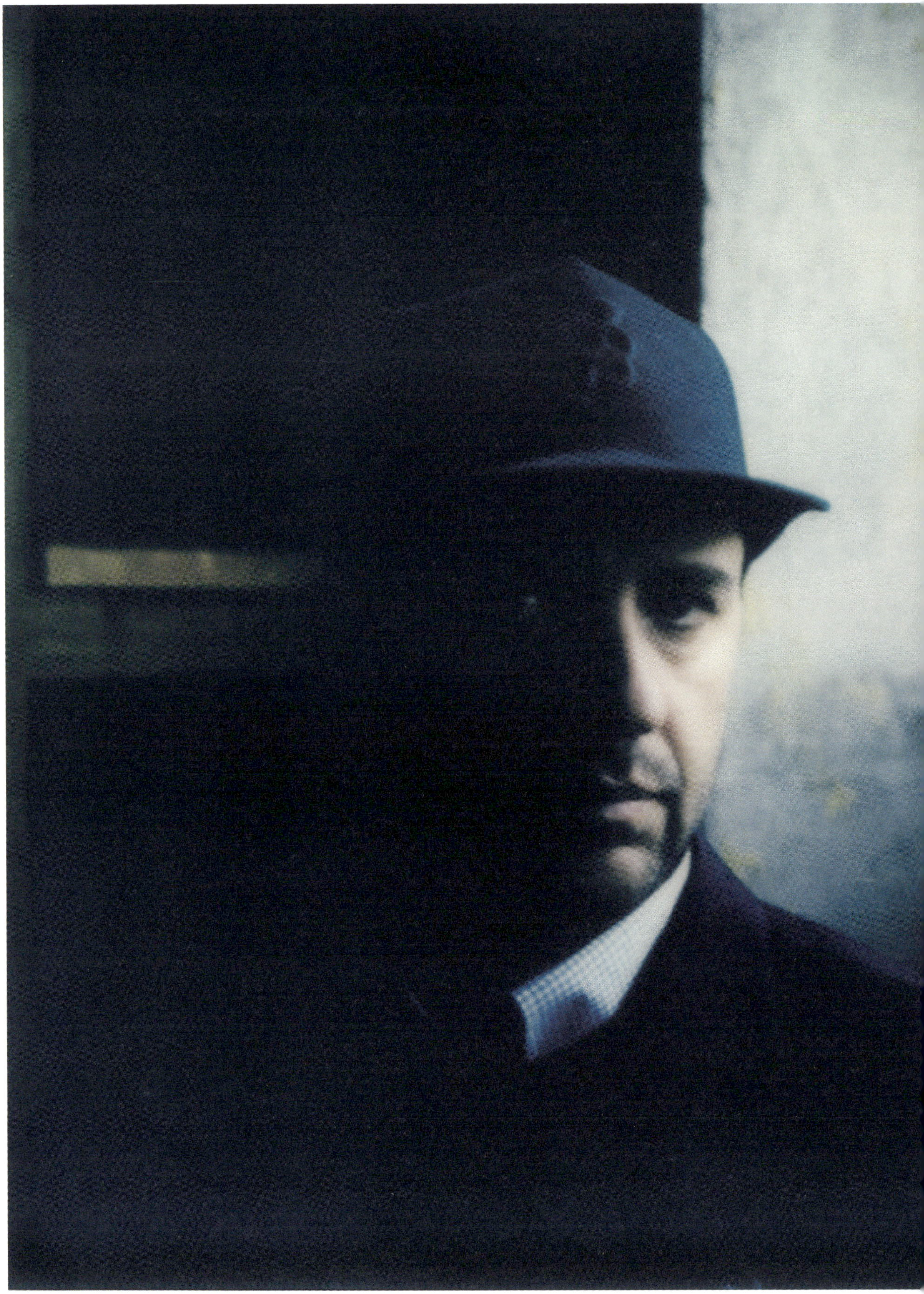

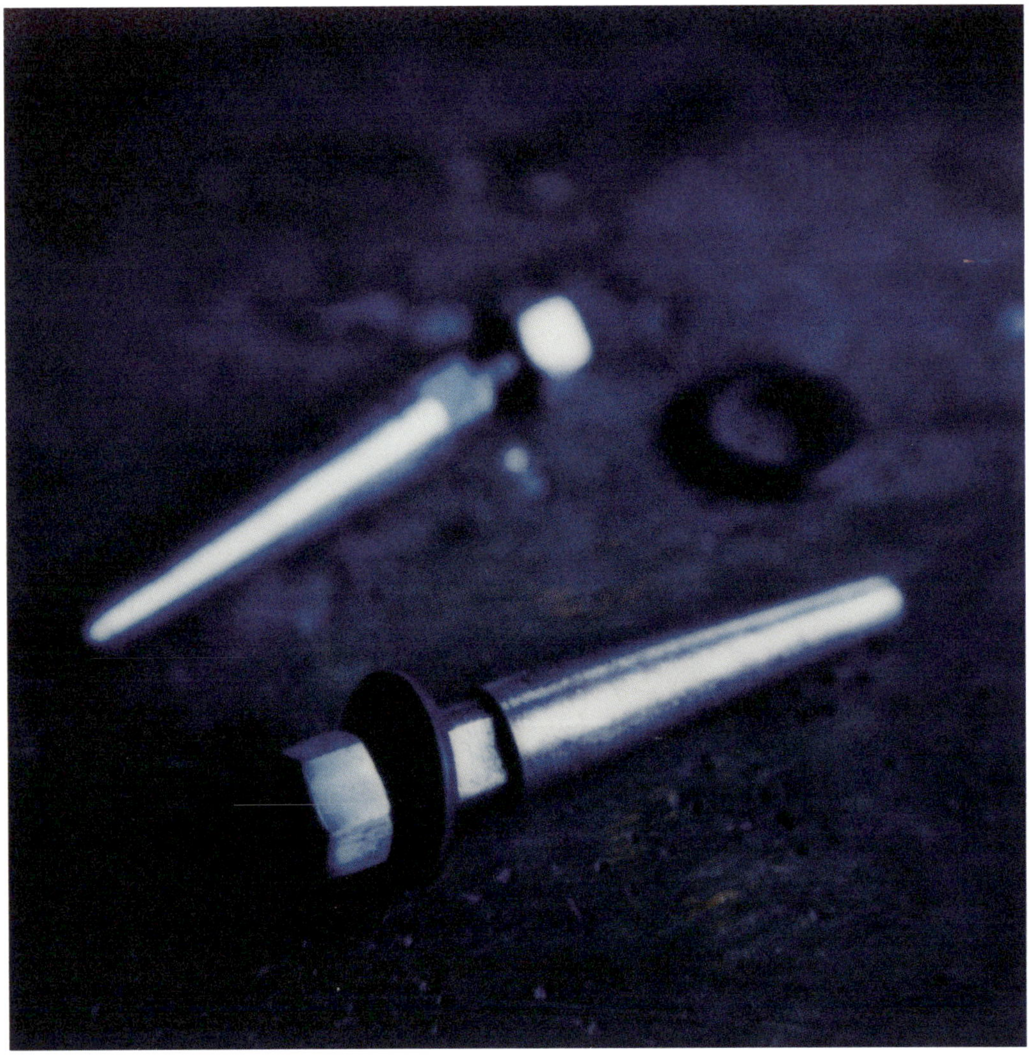

Bolts

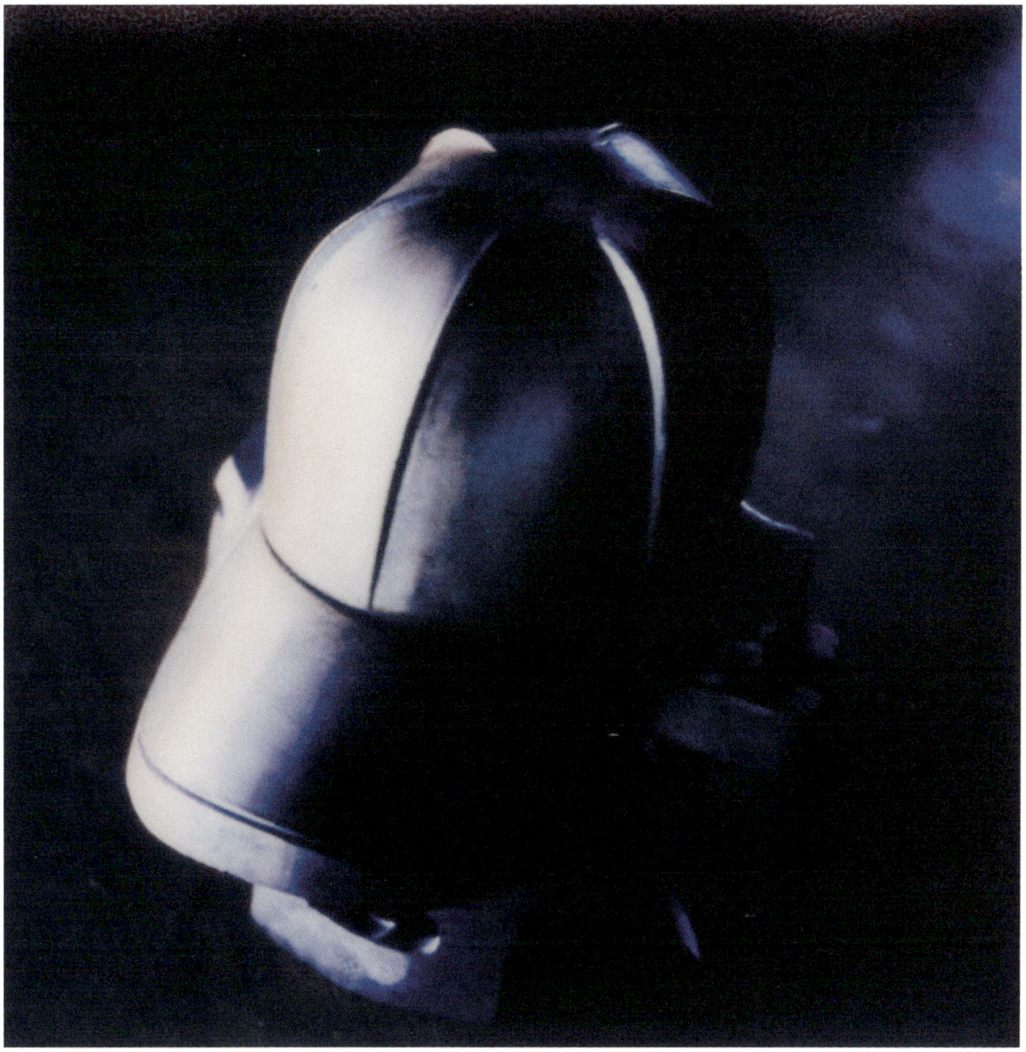

Aluminium baseball hat block

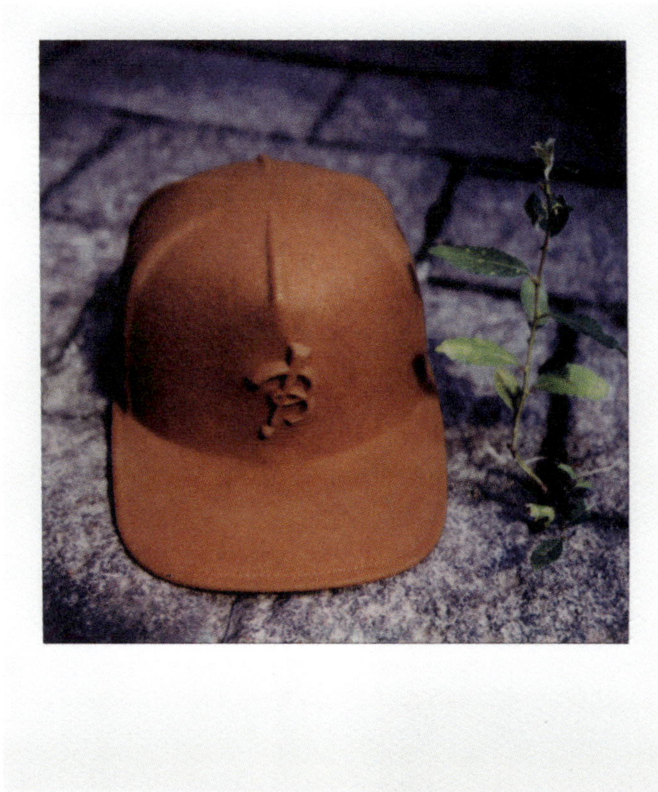

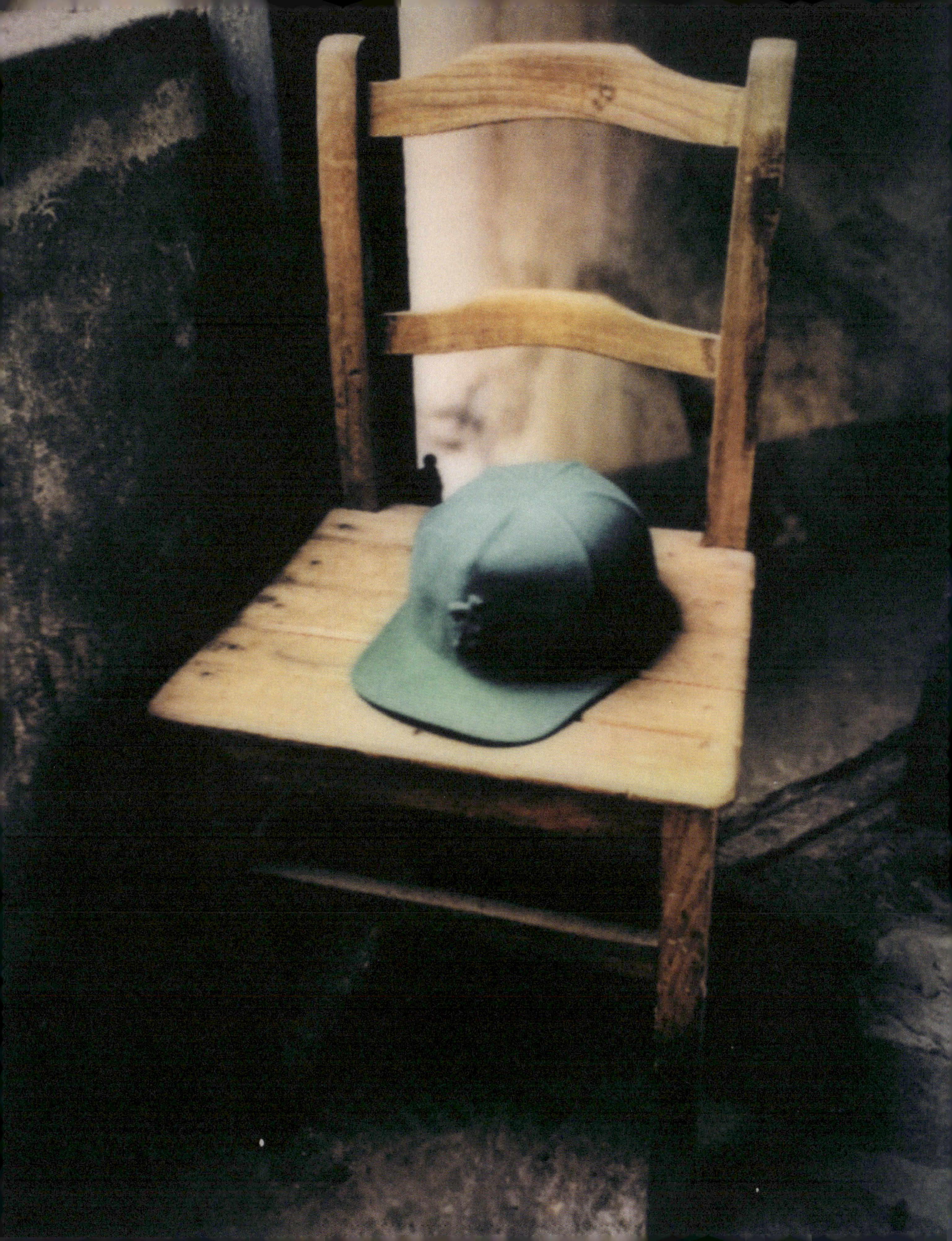

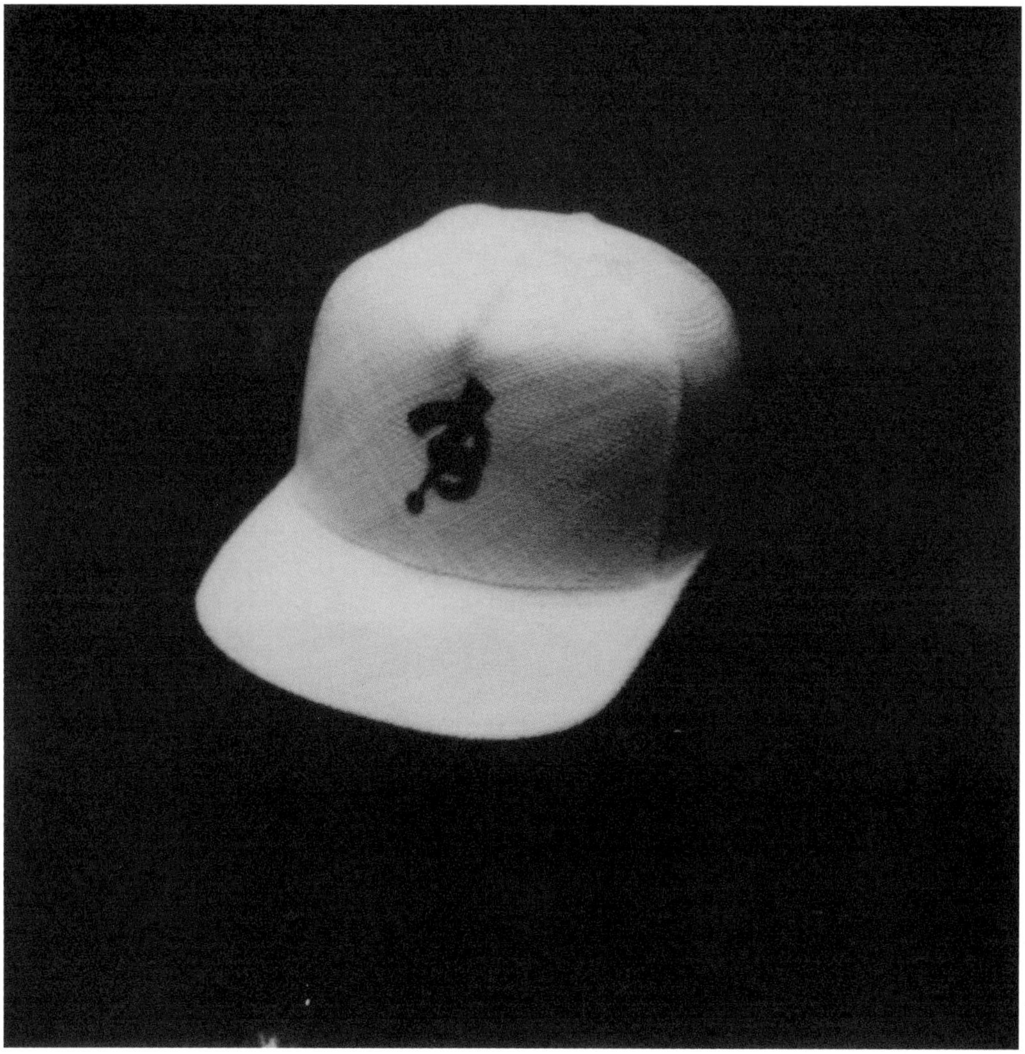

Tom in straw fiber

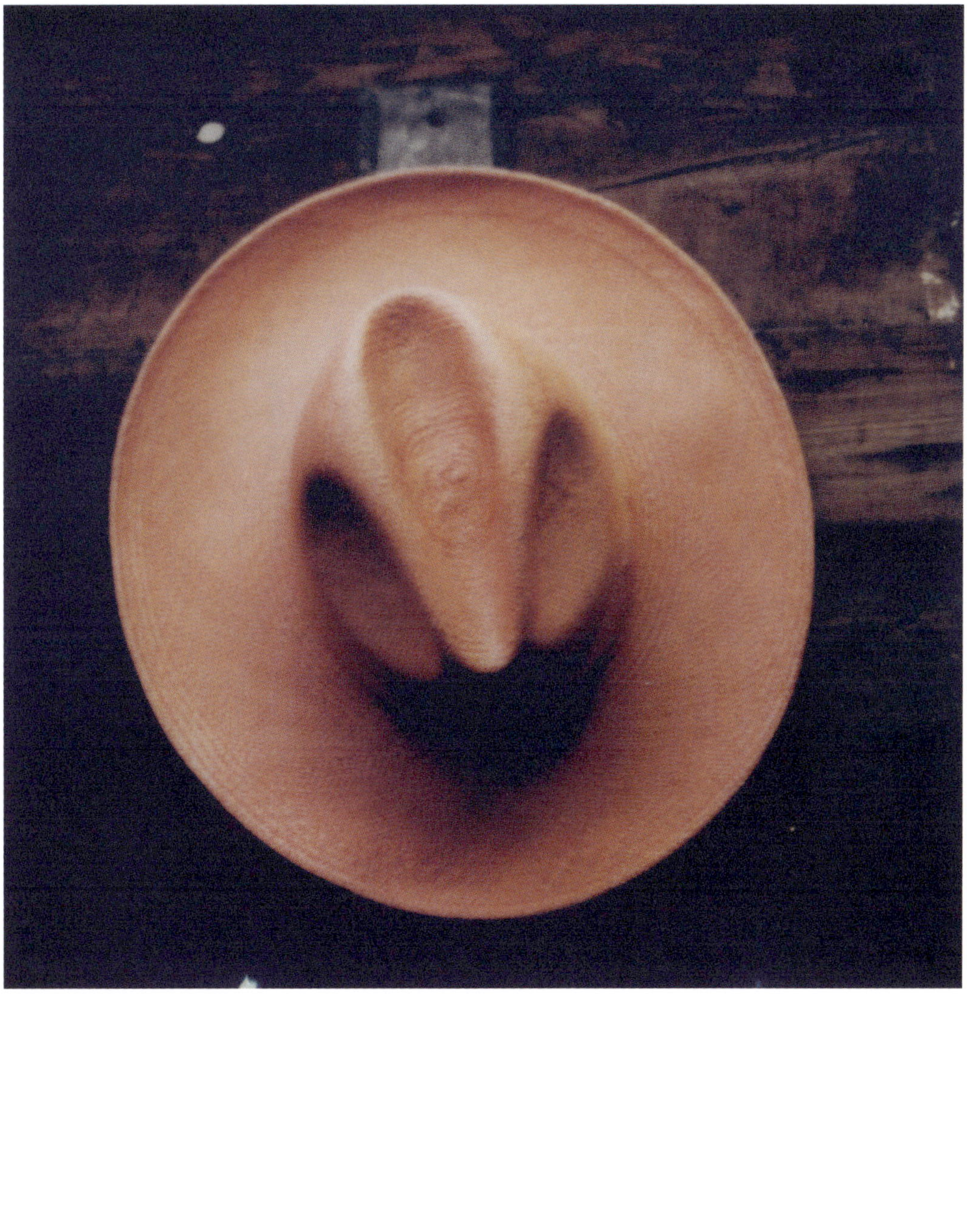

Steve, straw hat

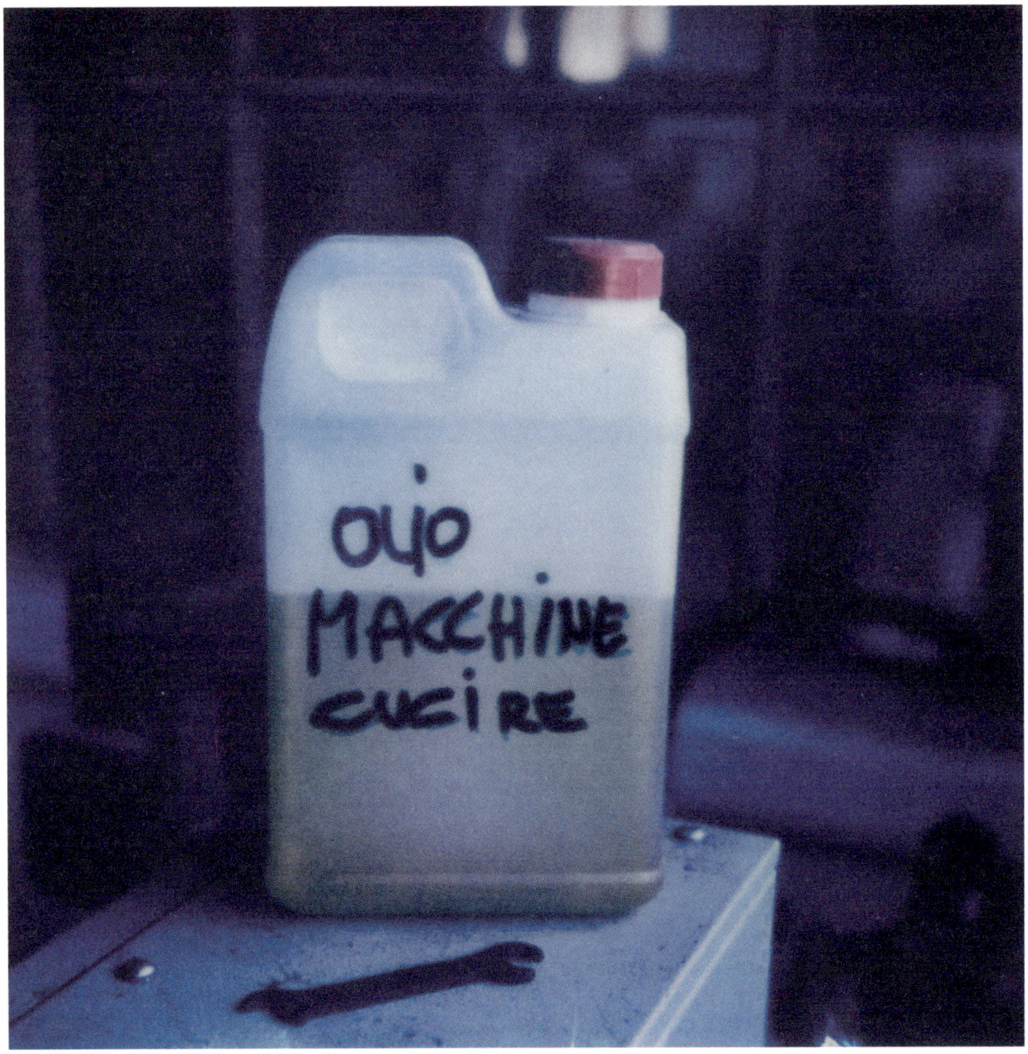

Oil tank for sewing machine

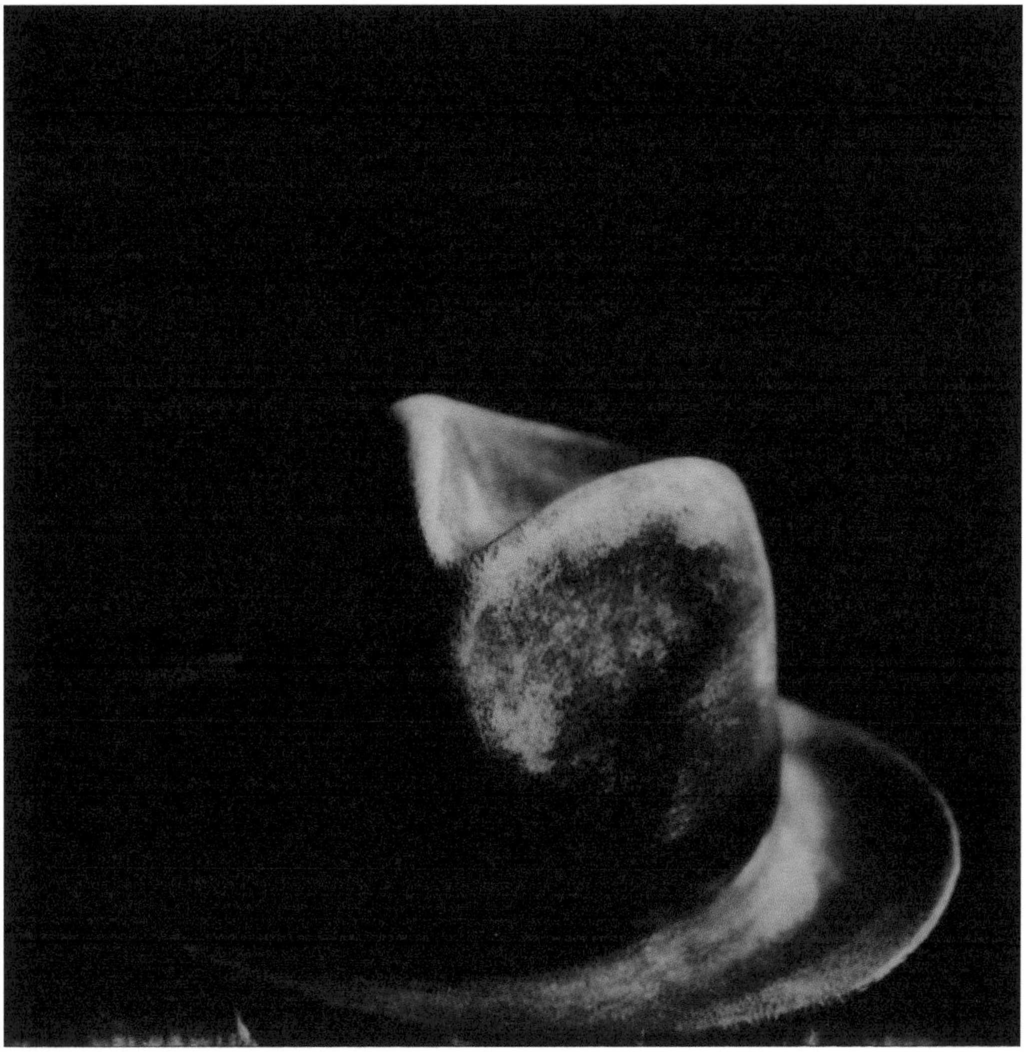

Stressed felt Fedora

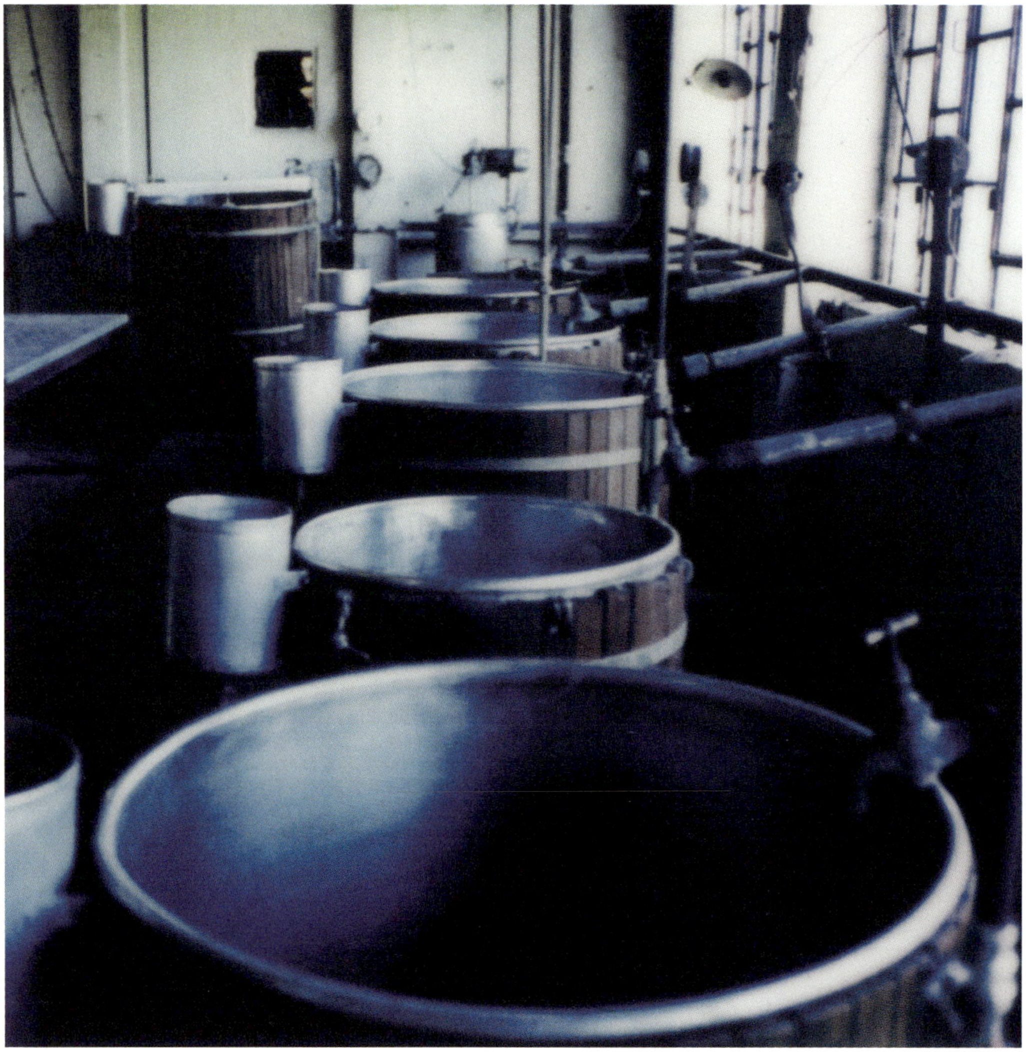

Dyeing vats

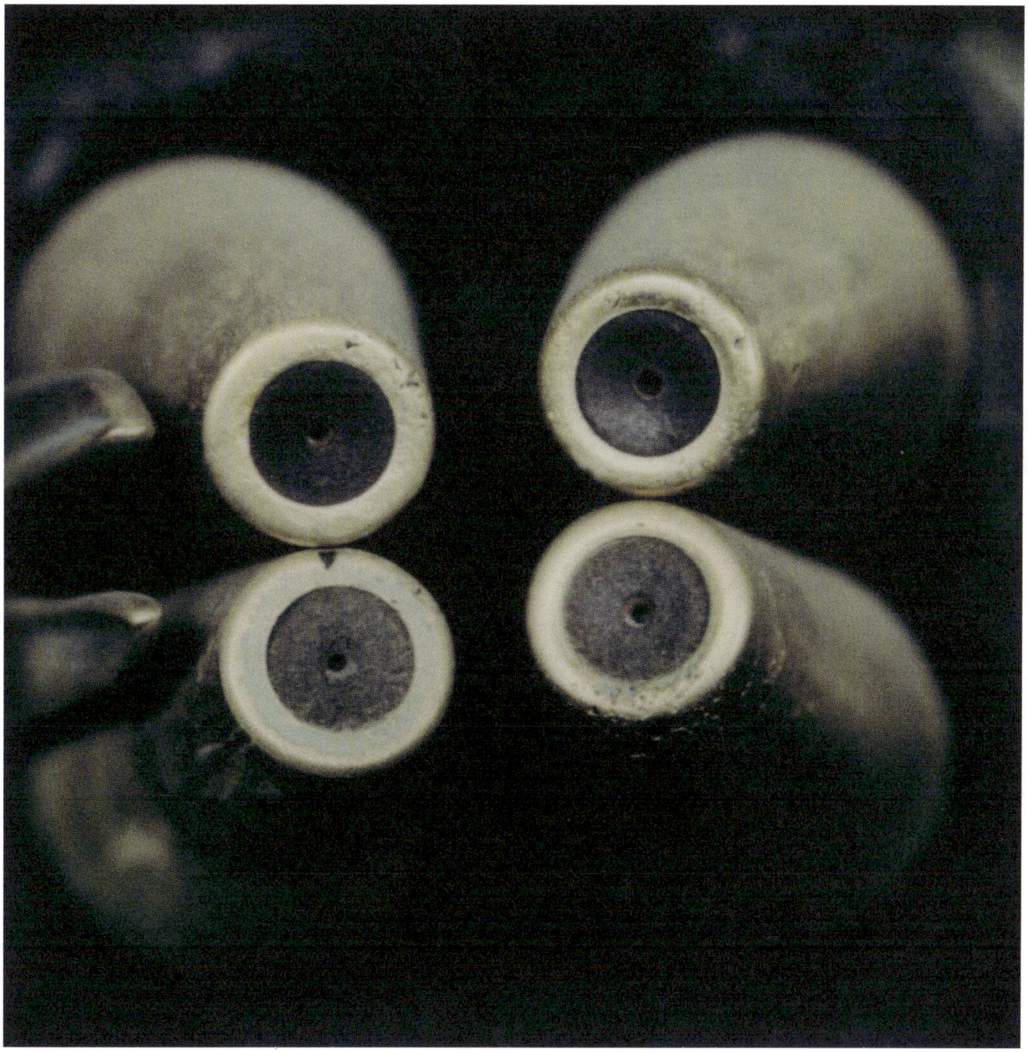

Rotating cones for molding felt hats

Bowler or Bombetta hat

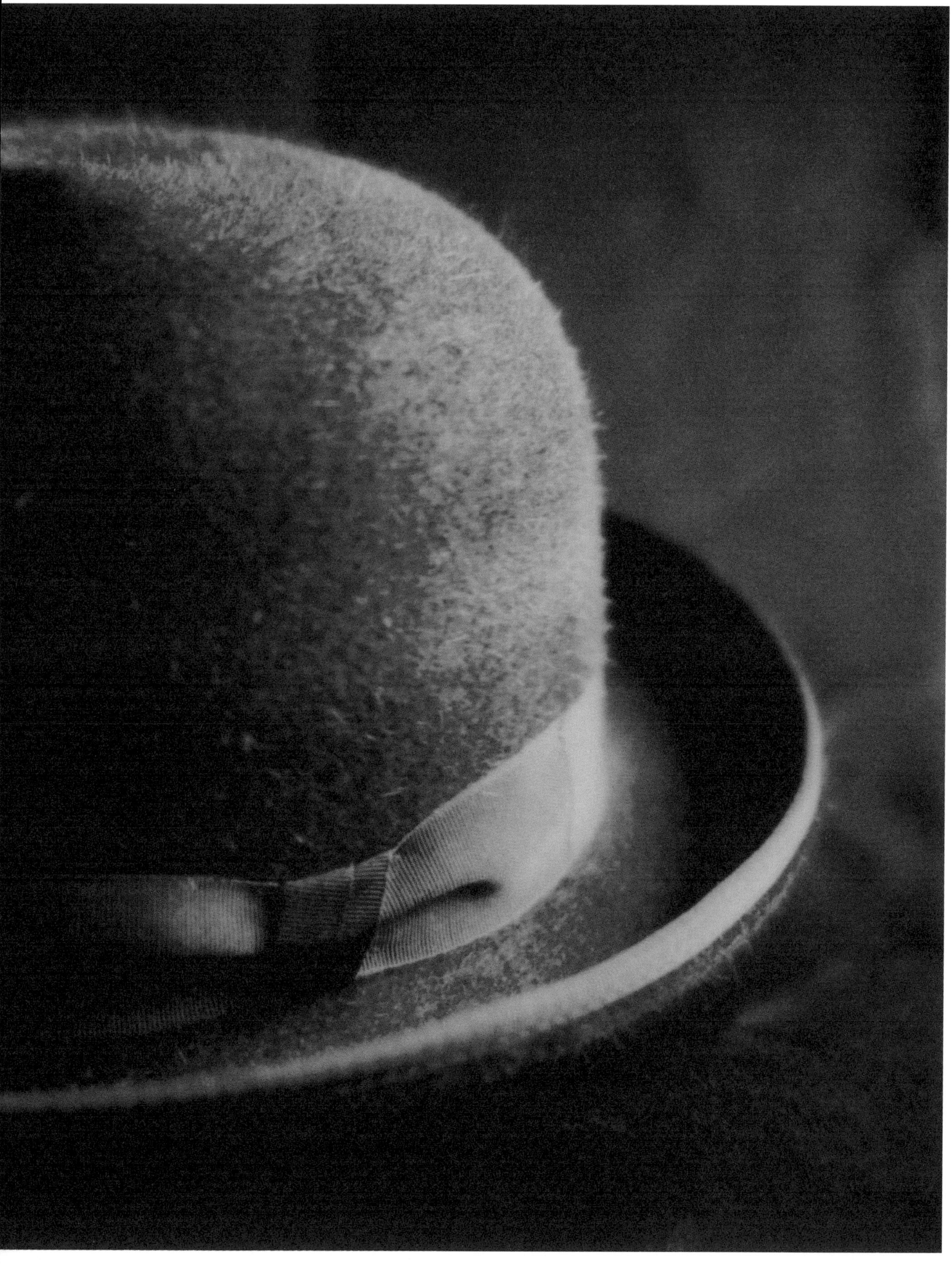

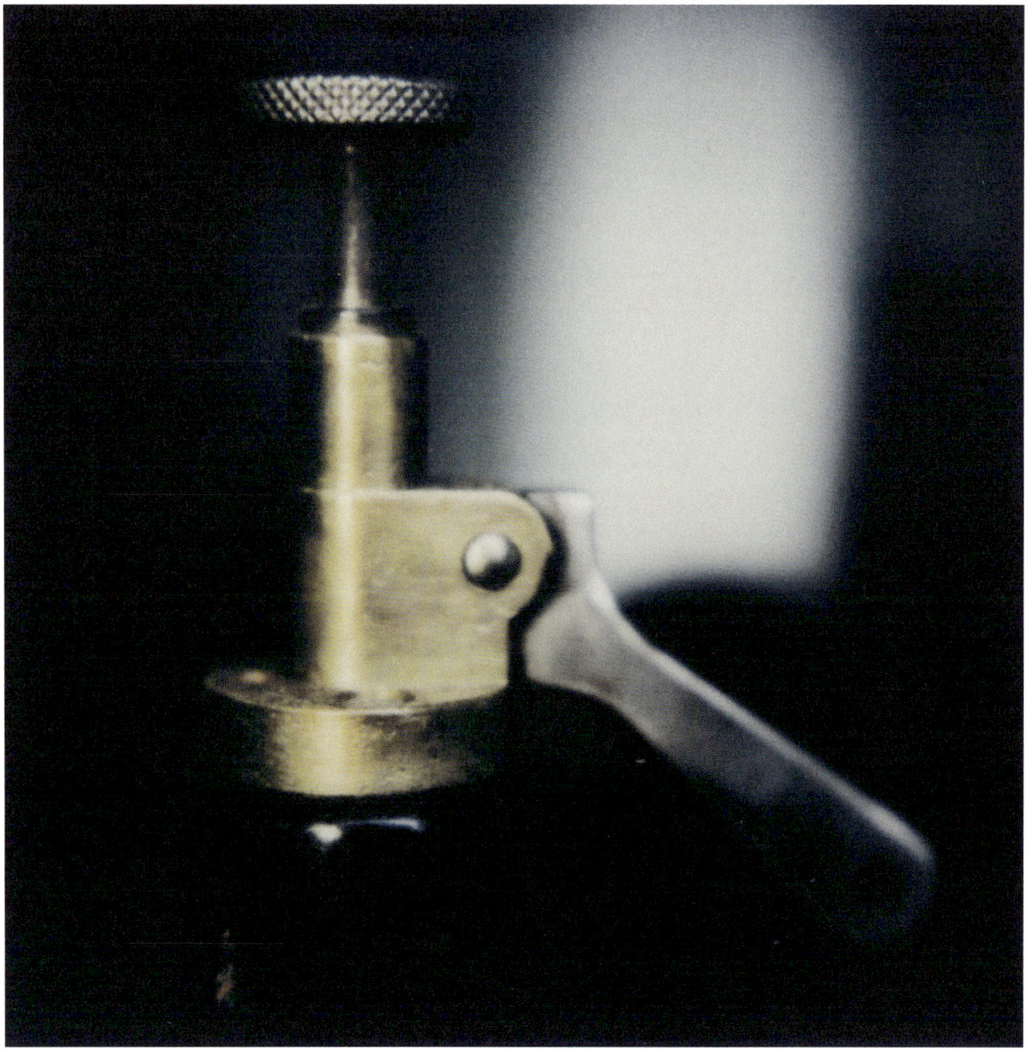

Hat block detail

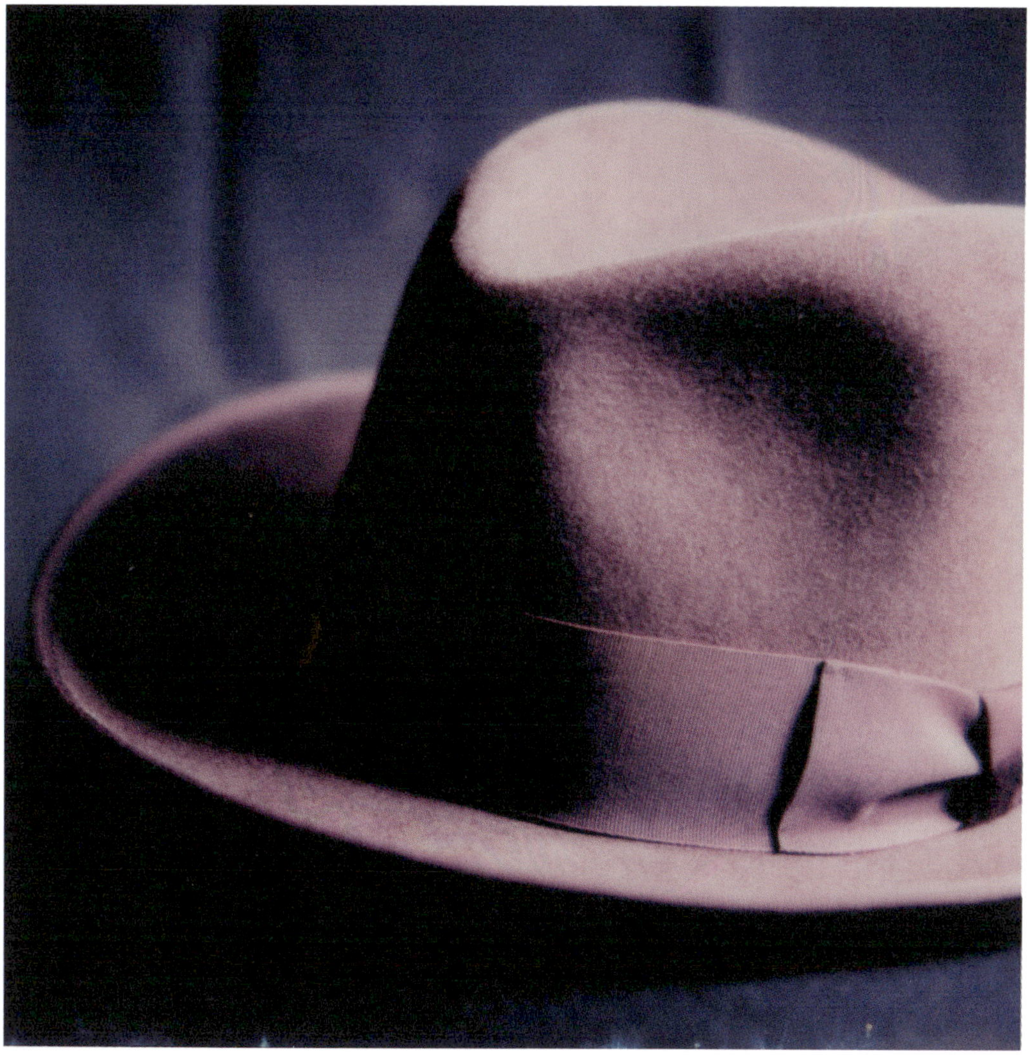

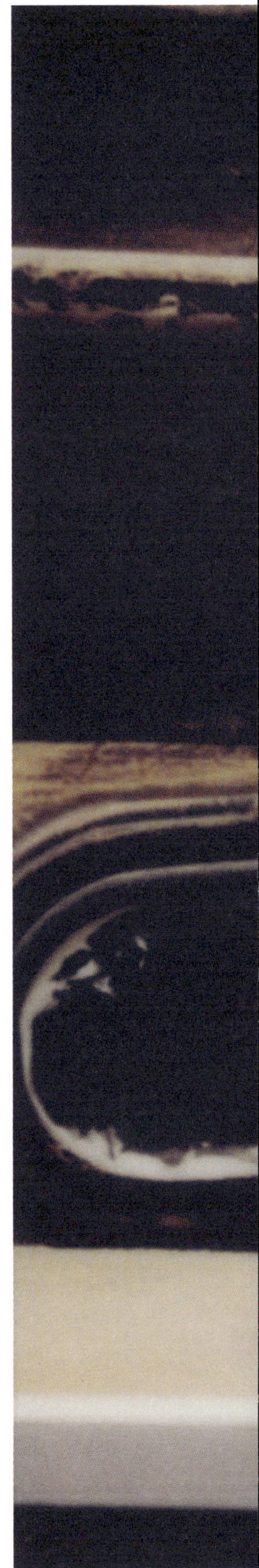

Blow-moulder, in the background

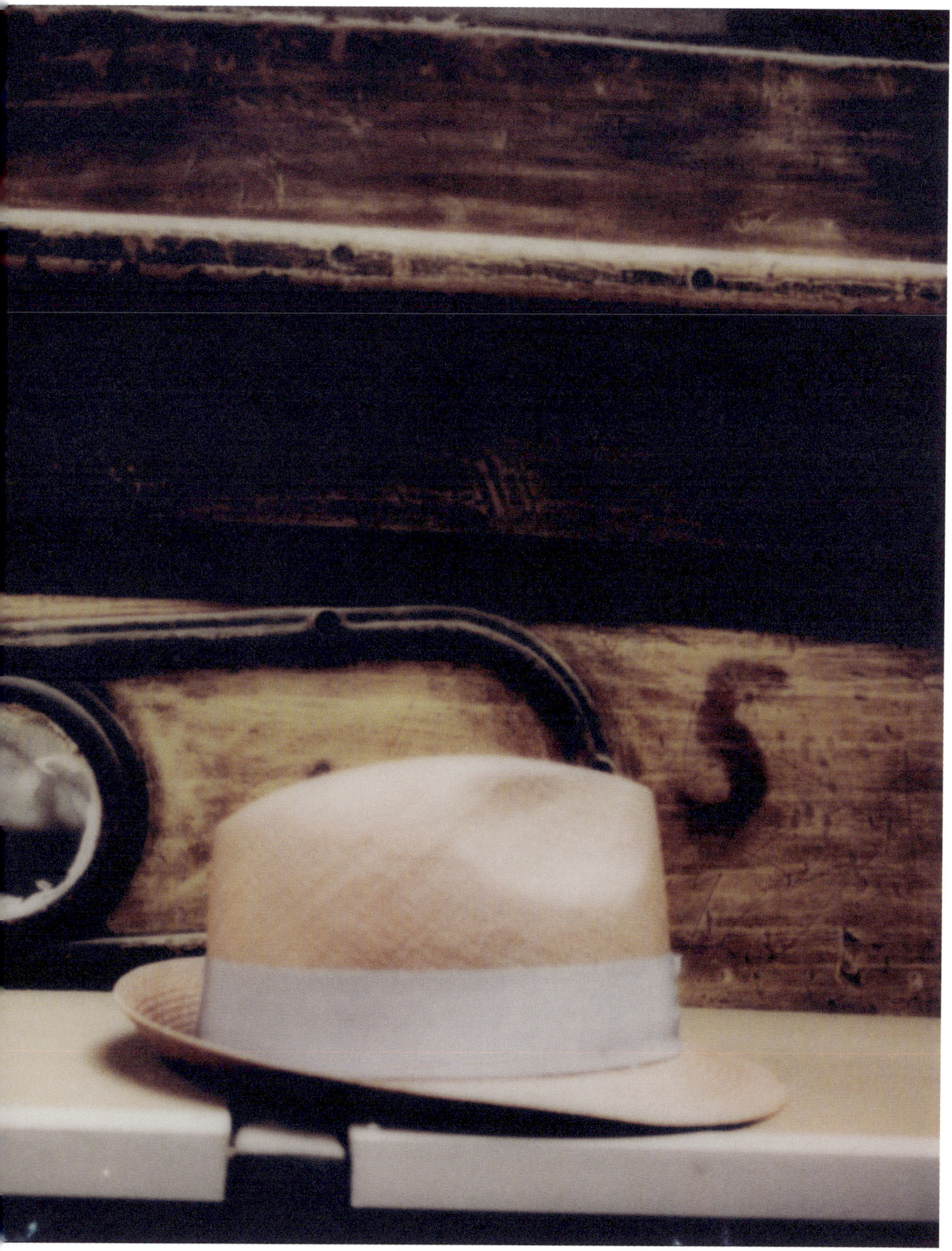

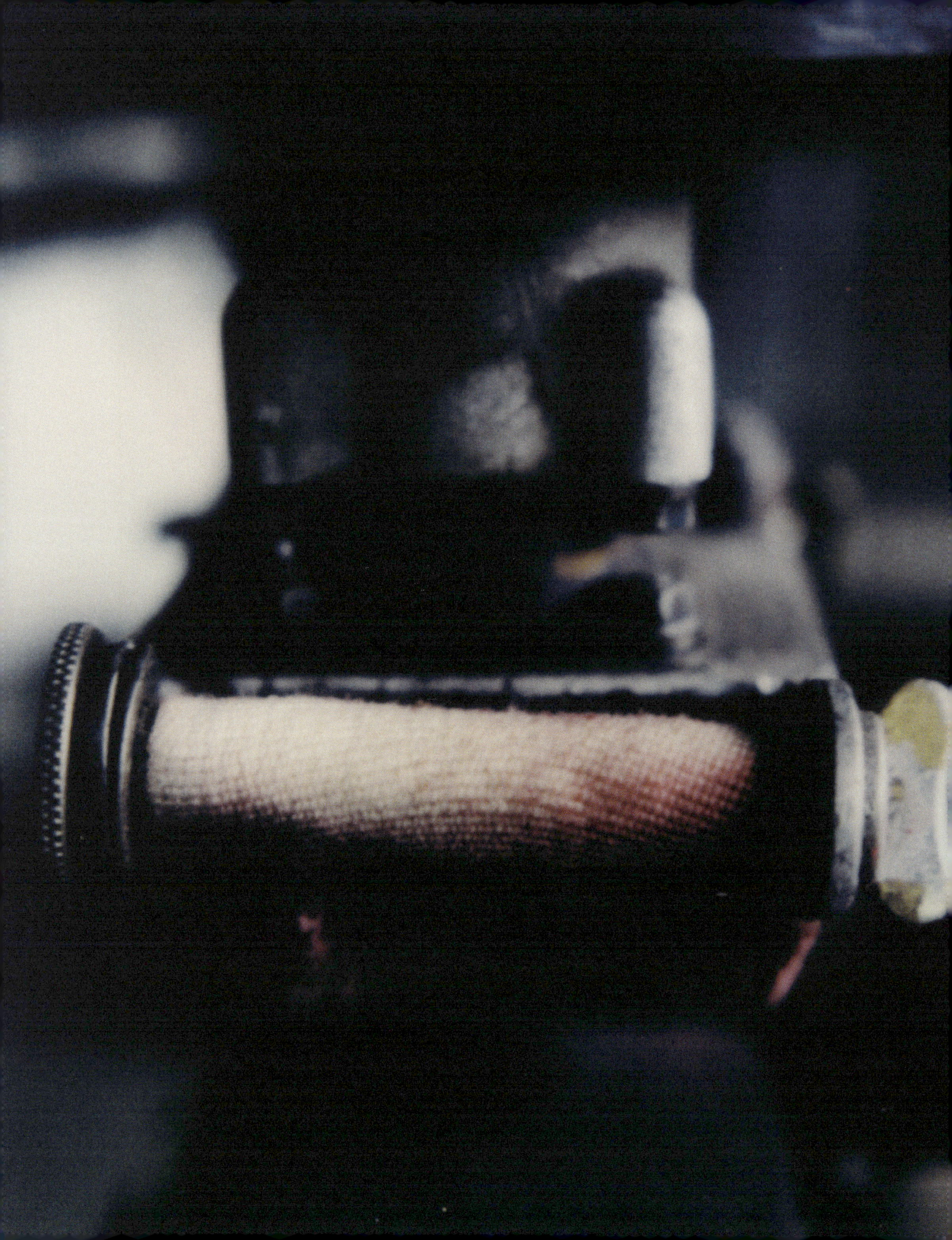

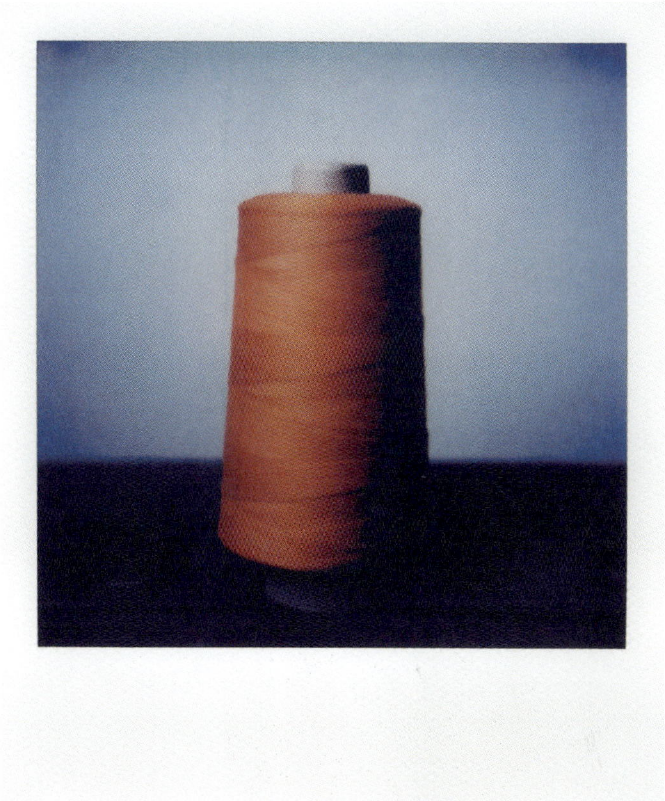

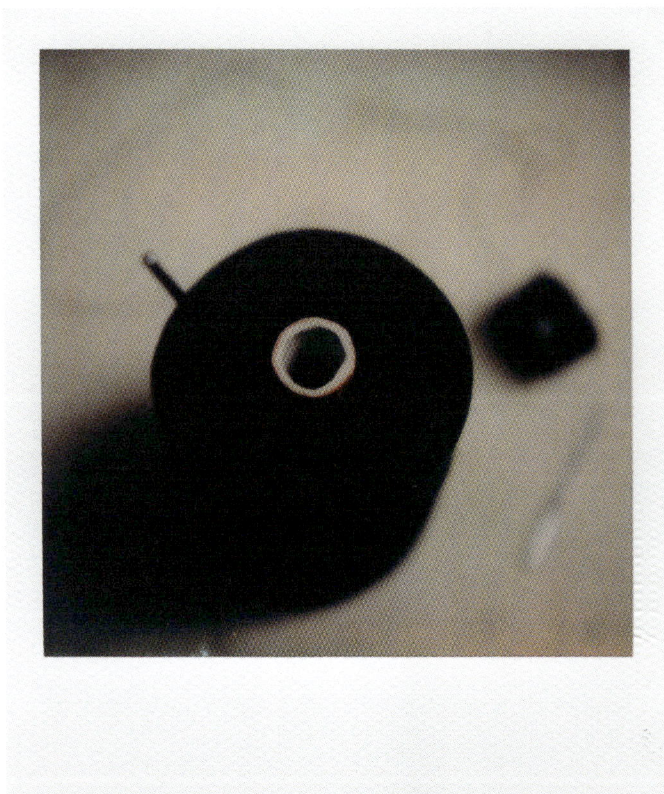

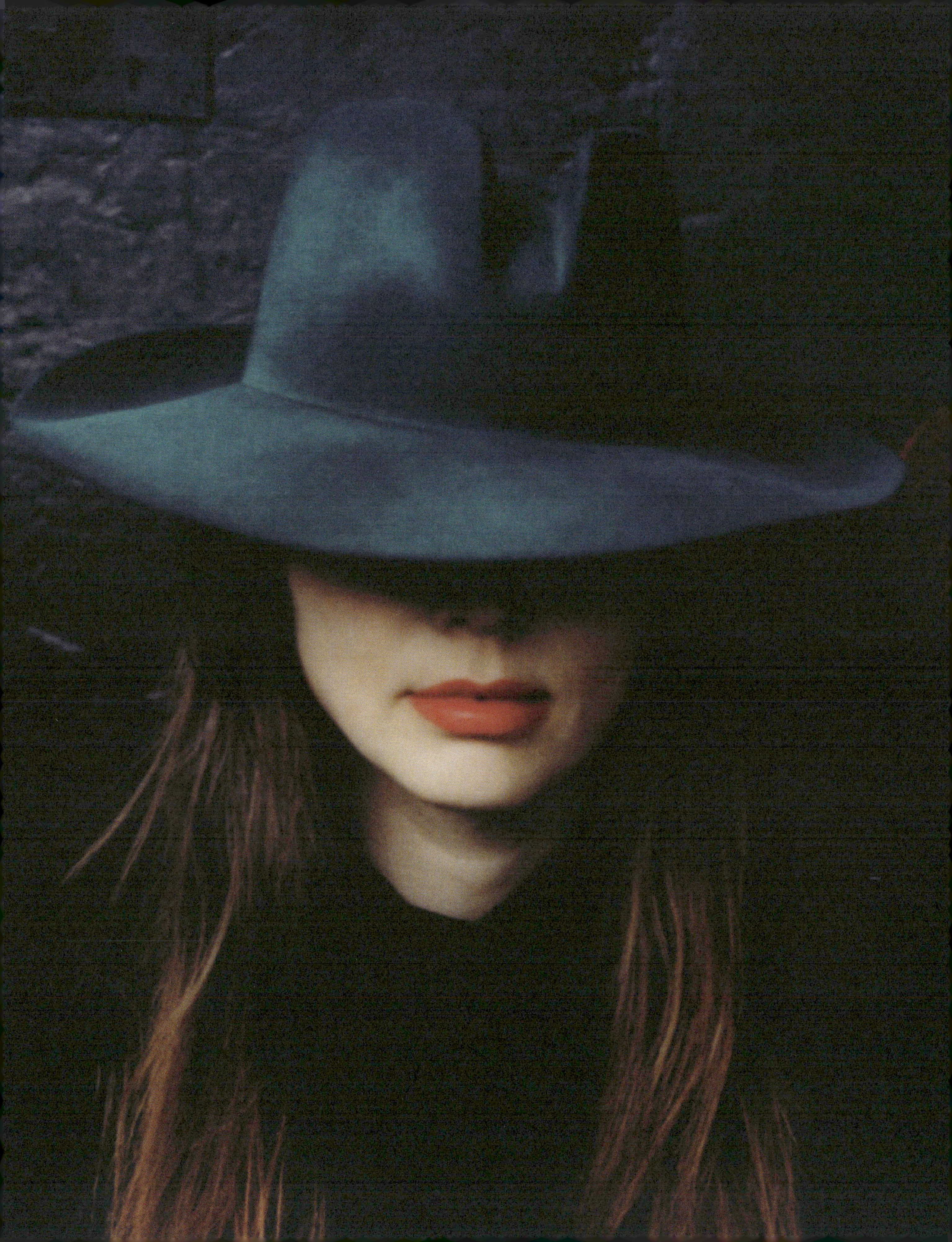

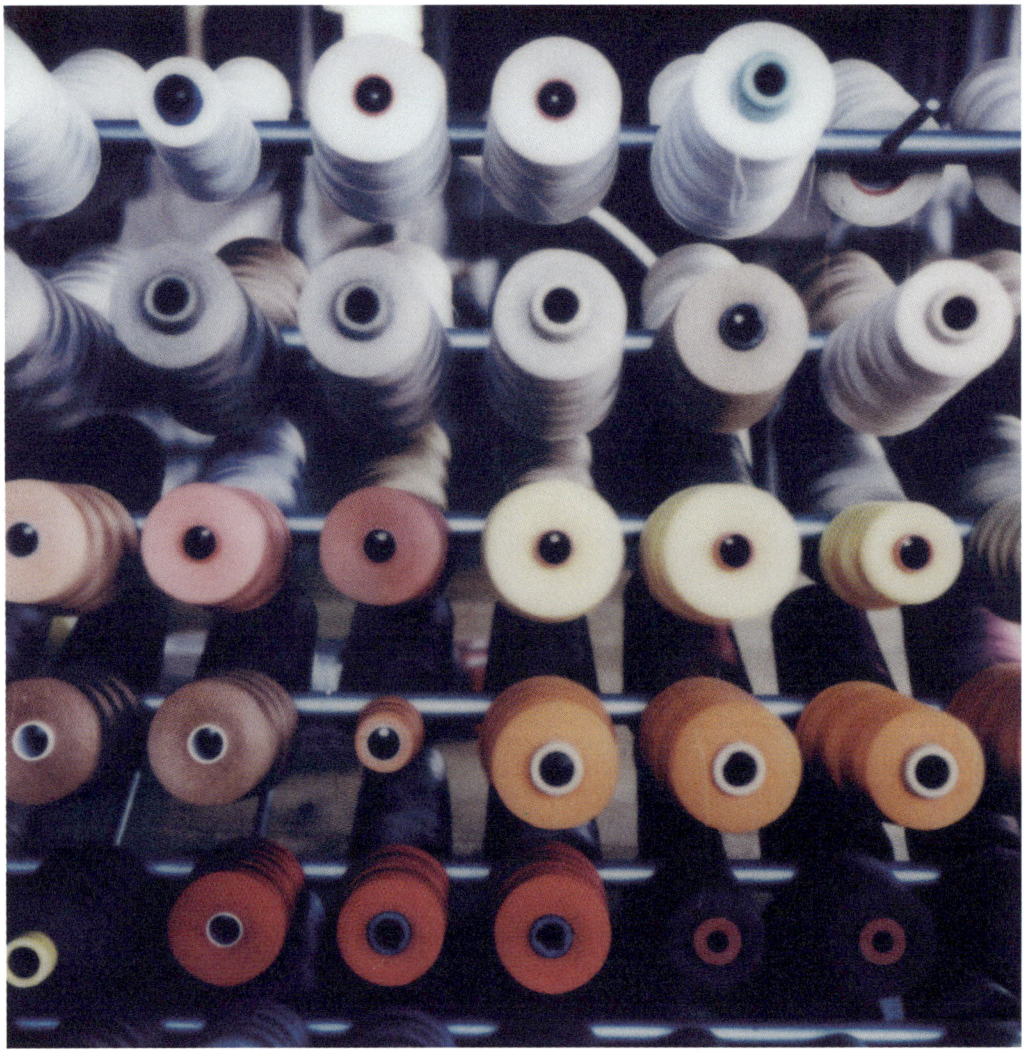

Reels of thread

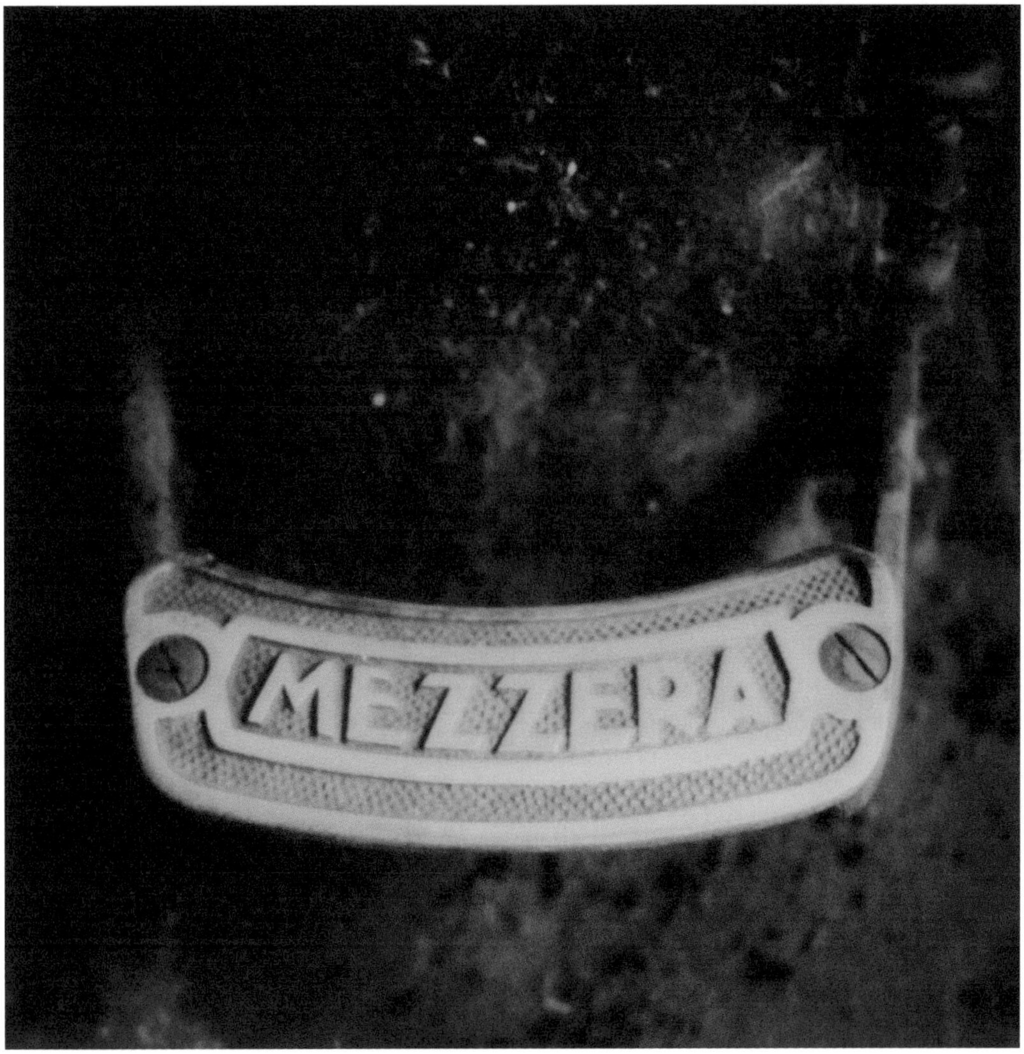

Mezzera footswitch

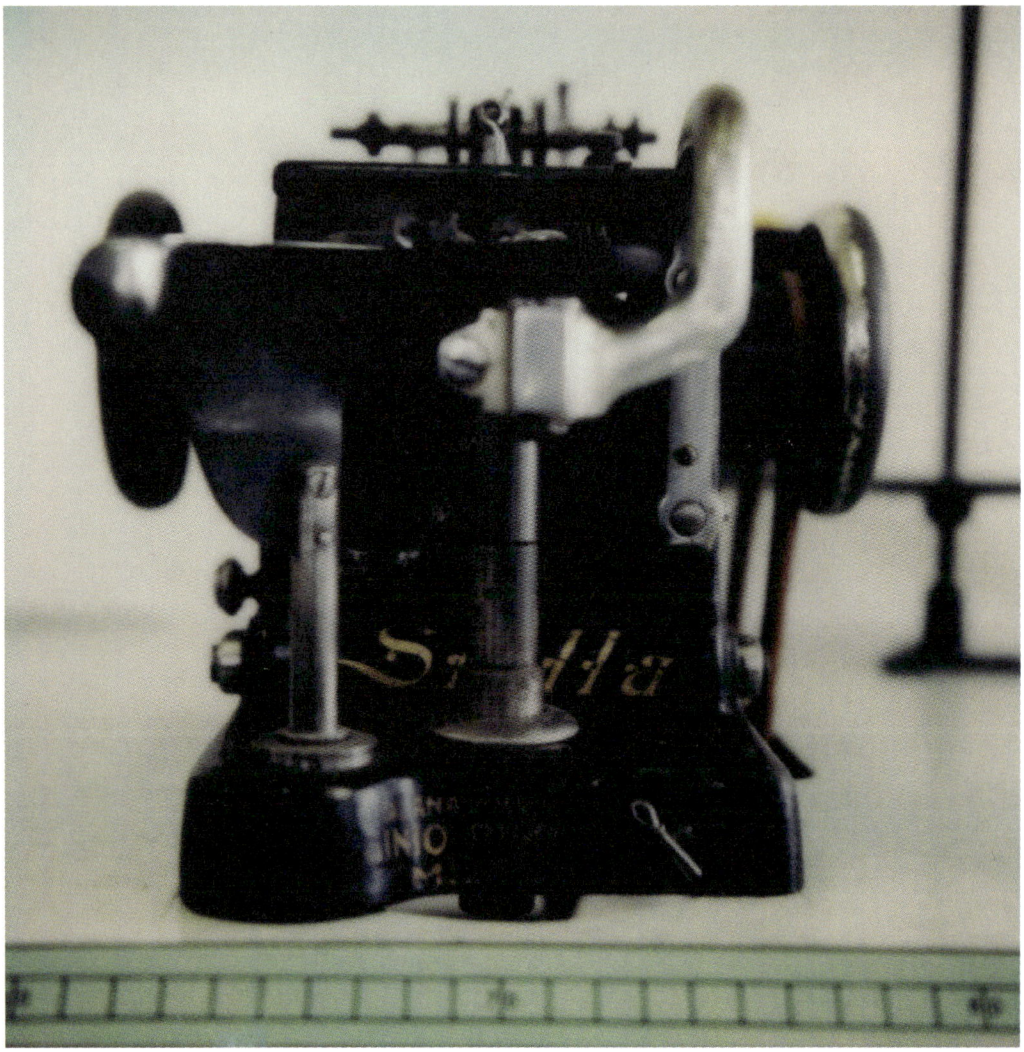

Sewing machine

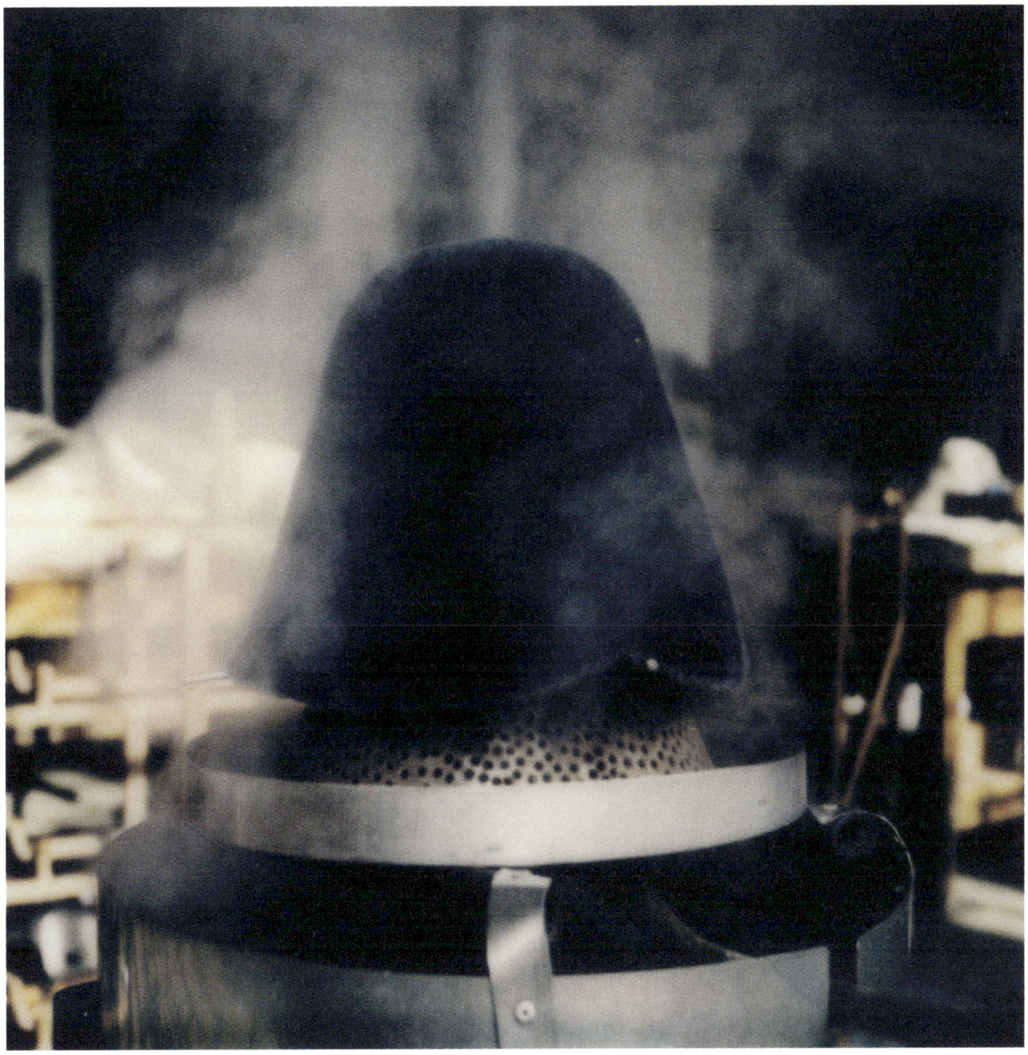

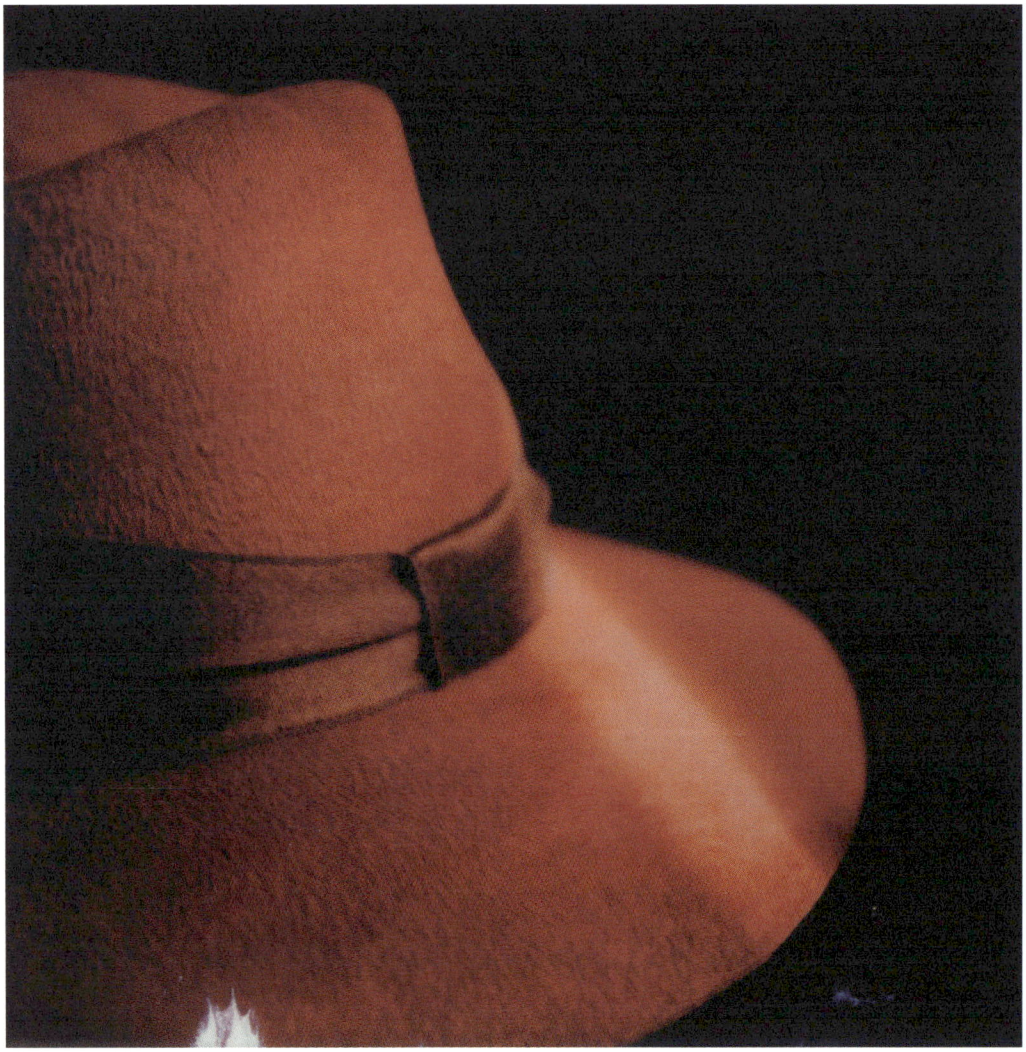

Red Behati in velour felt

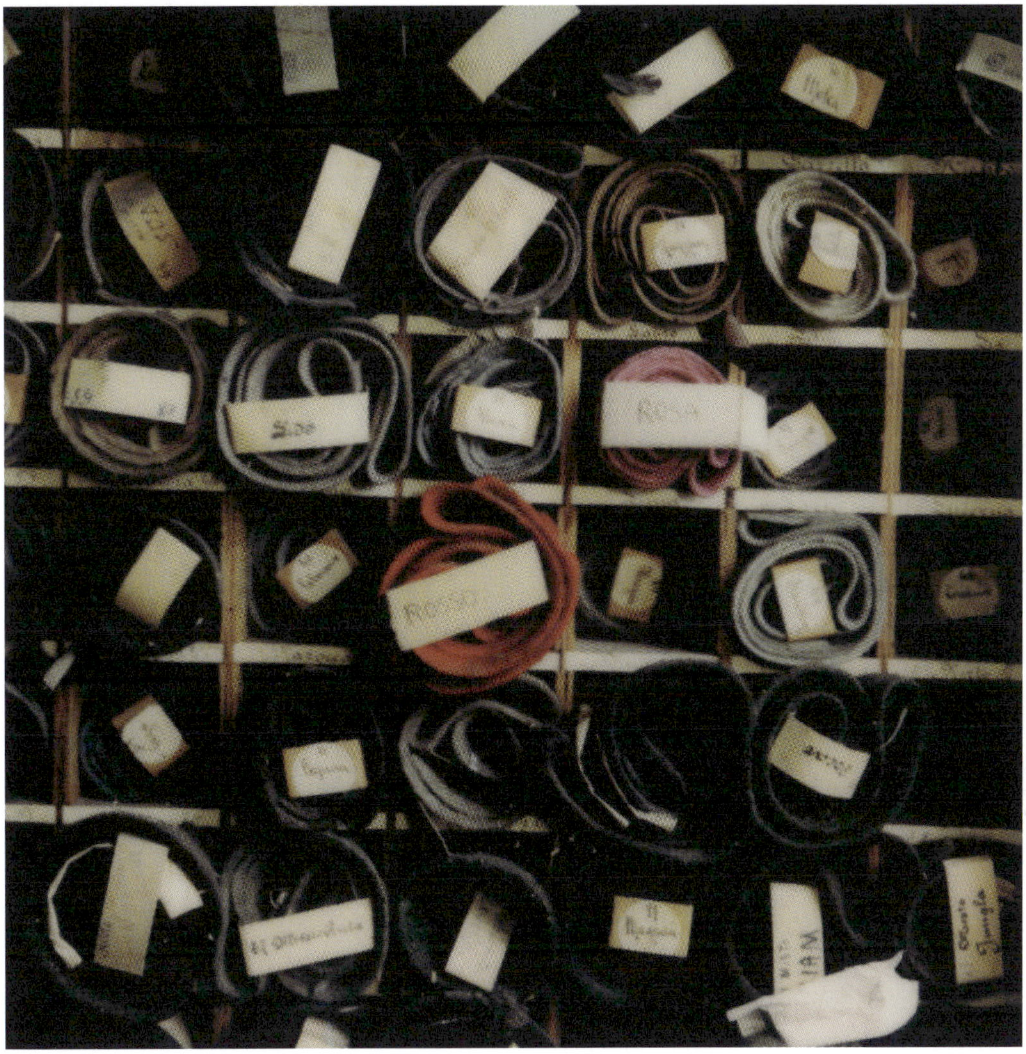
ROSA
ROSSO

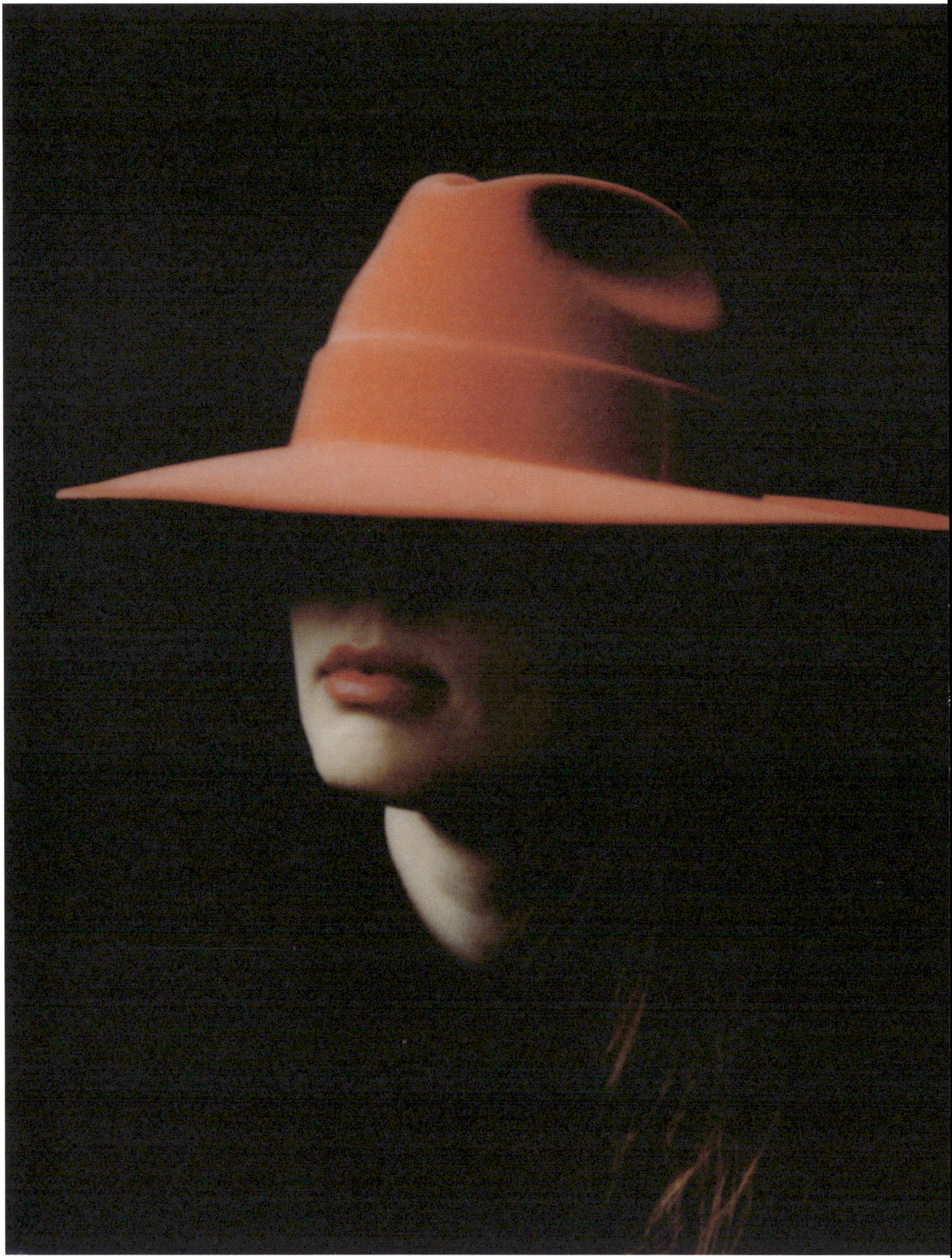

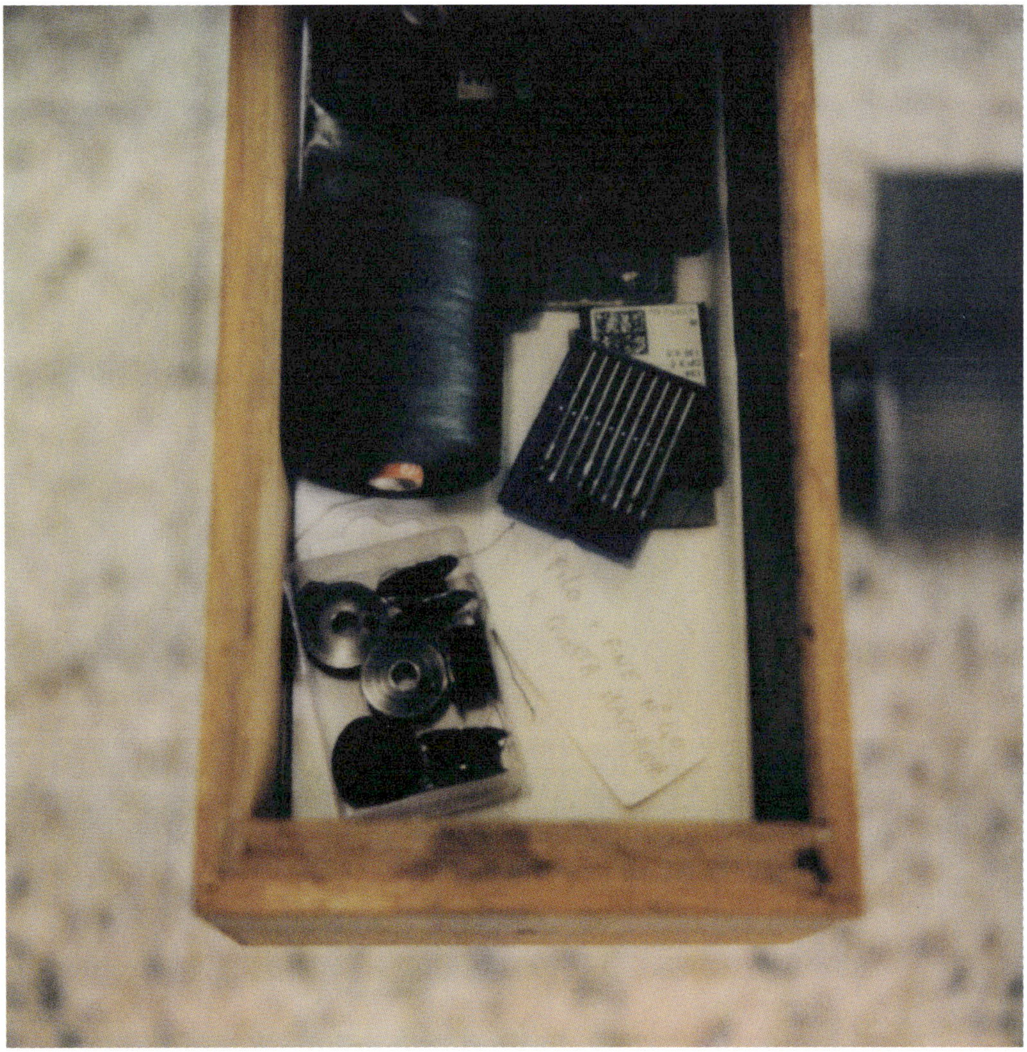

Sewing tools

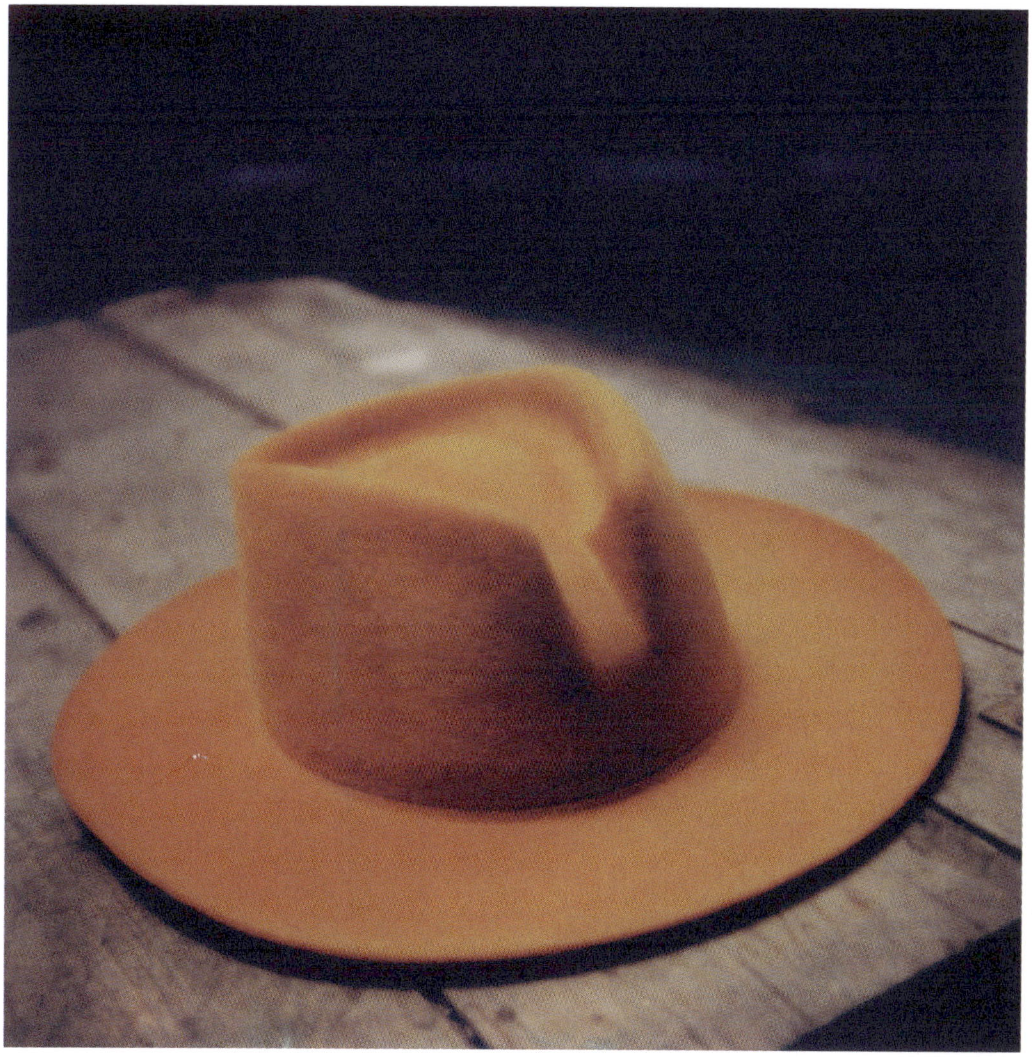

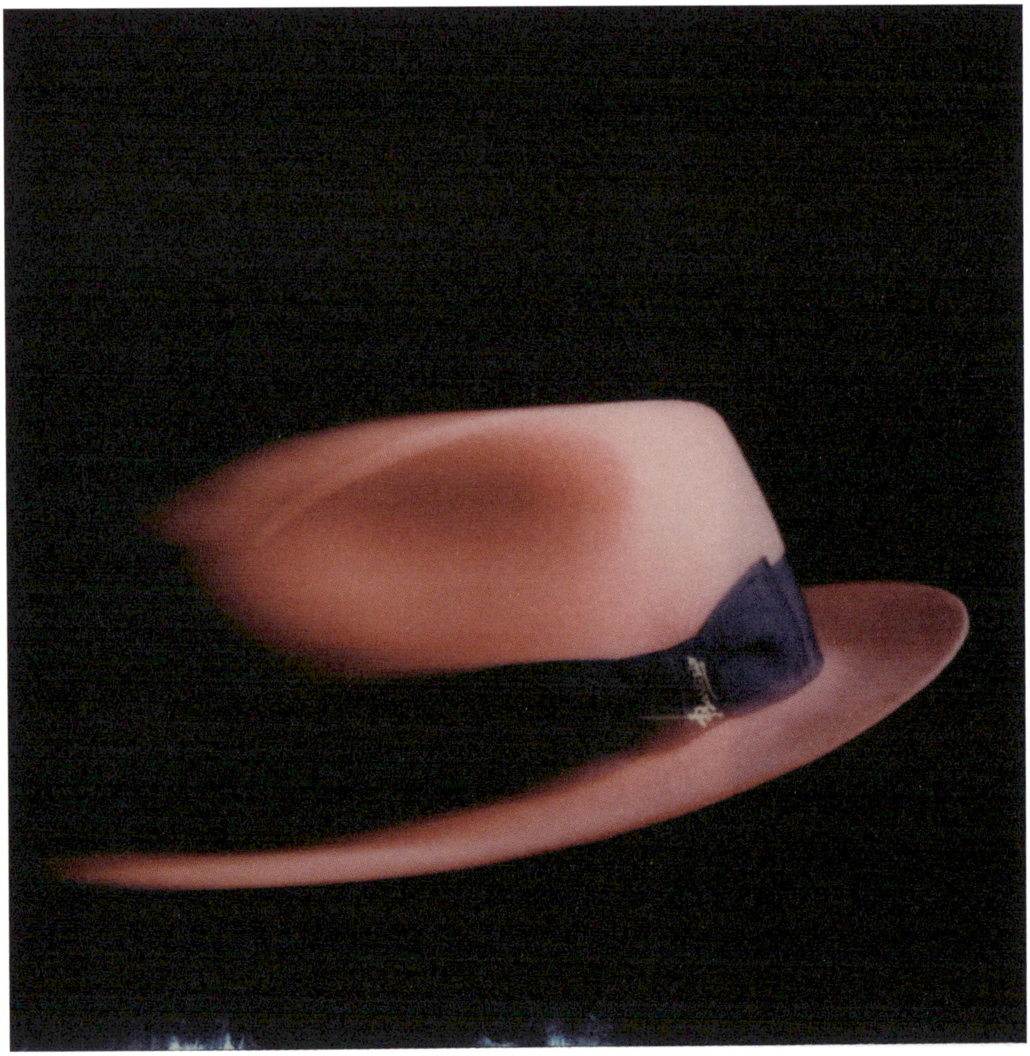

Low Fedora hat

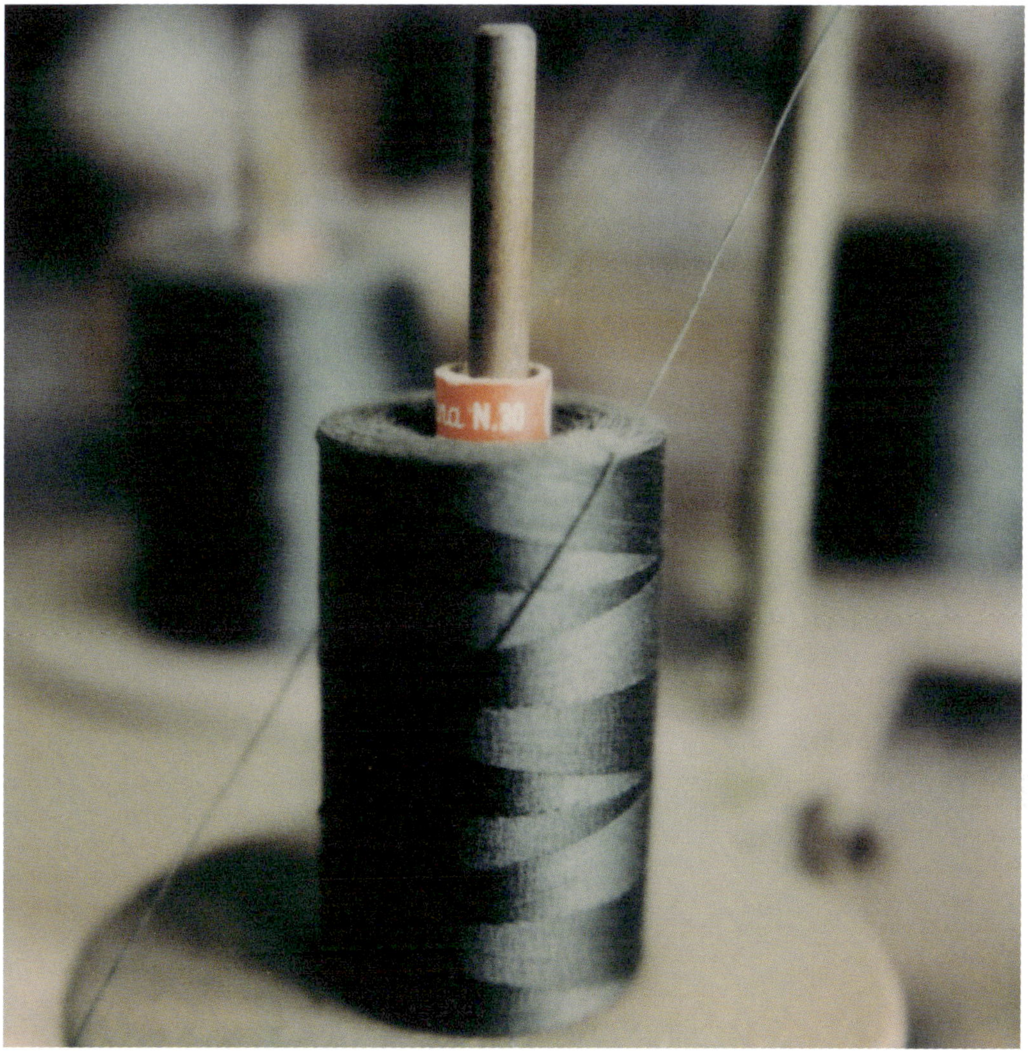

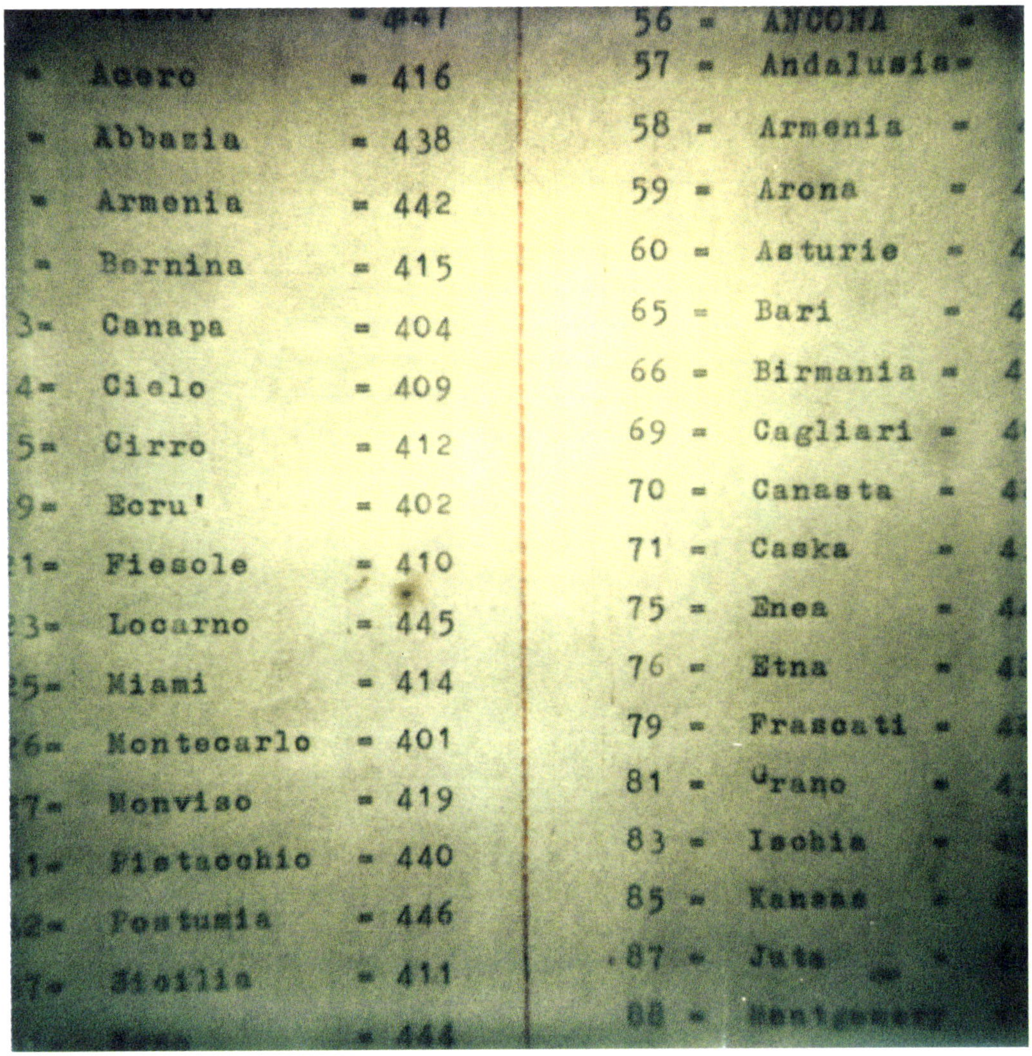

Colour card caption

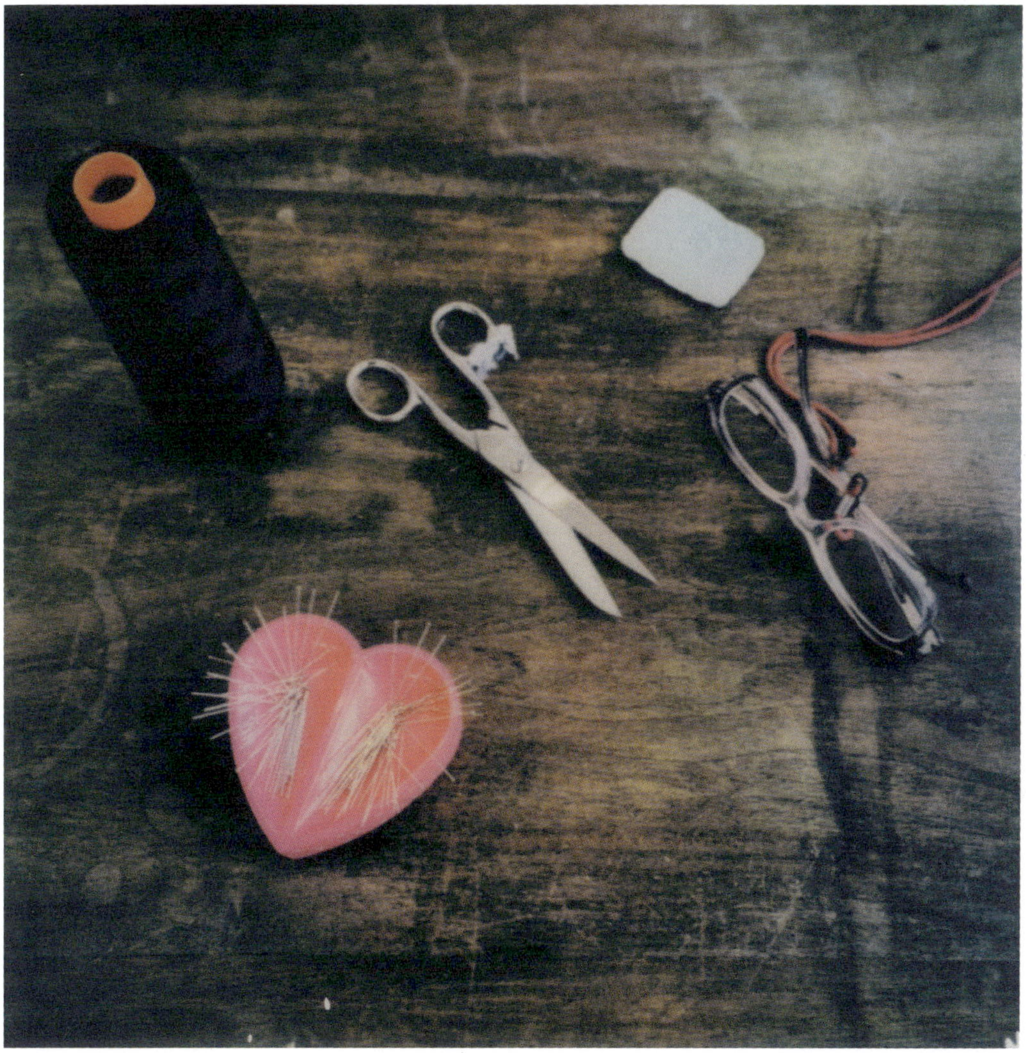

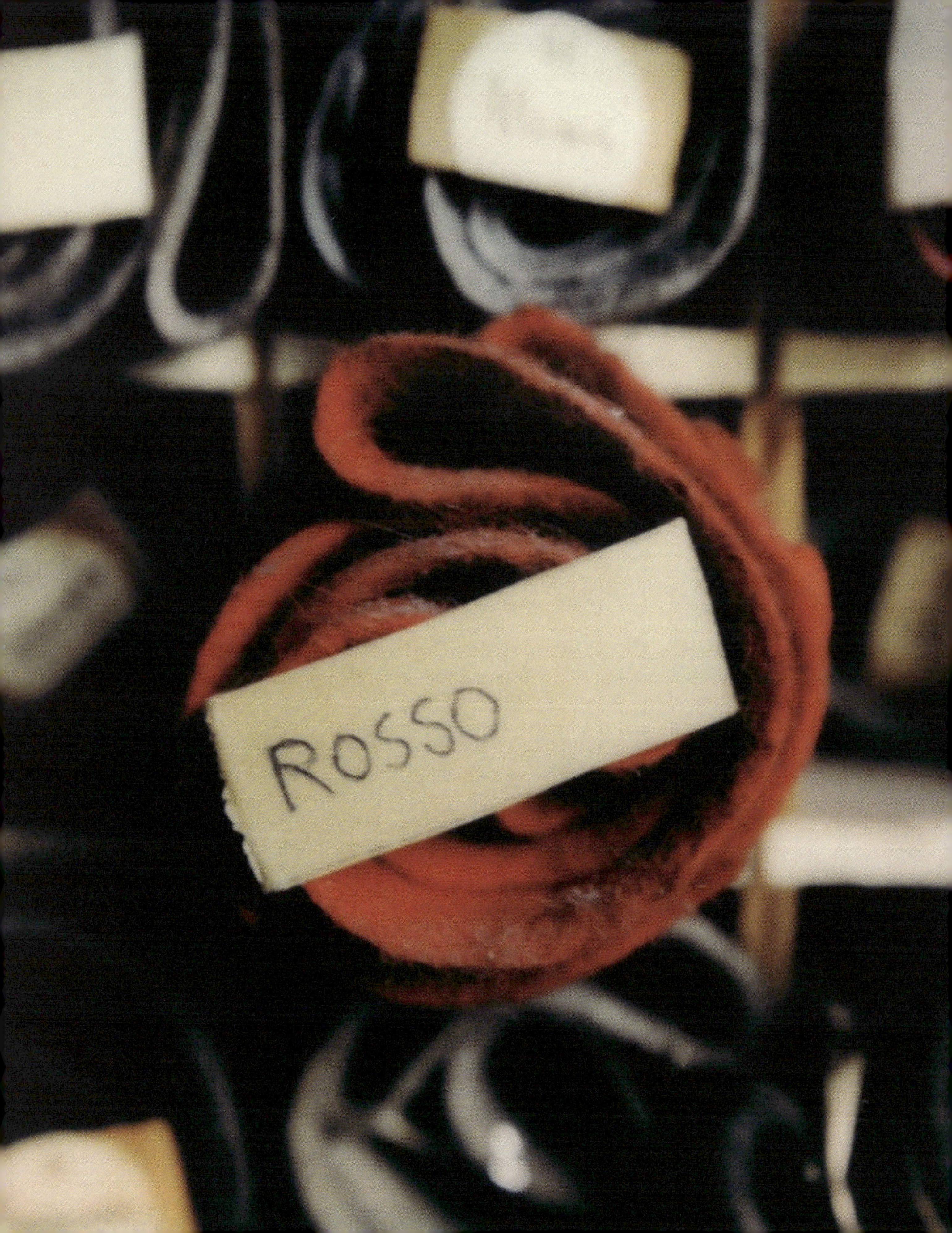
ROSSO

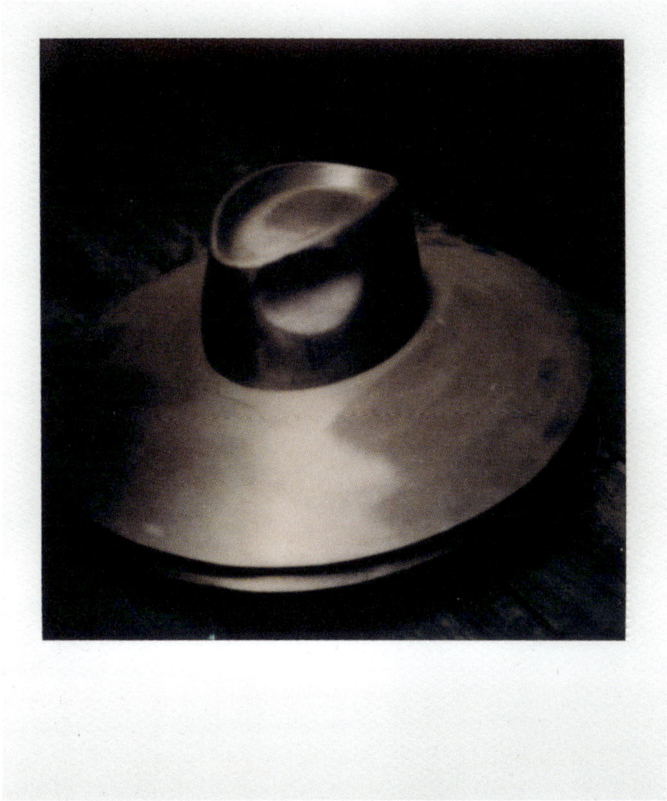

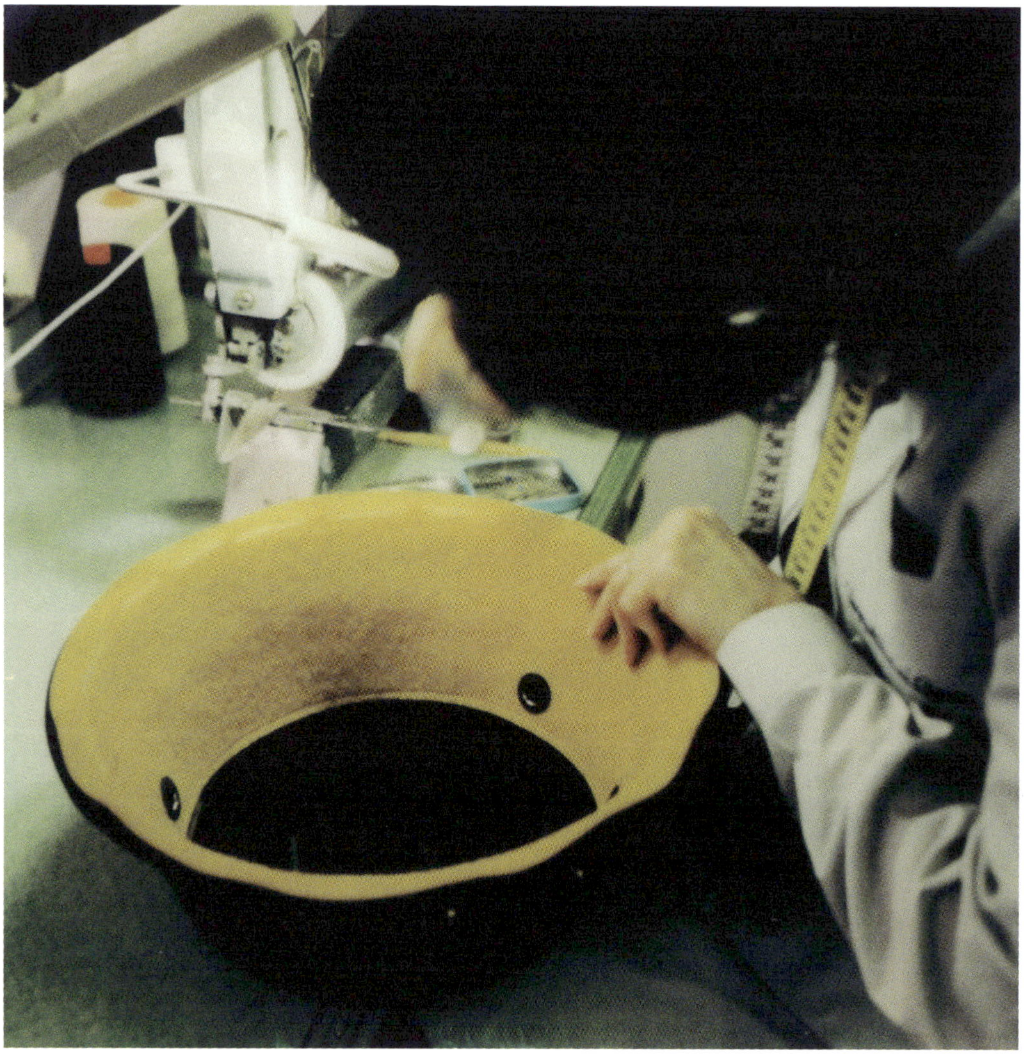

Seamstress

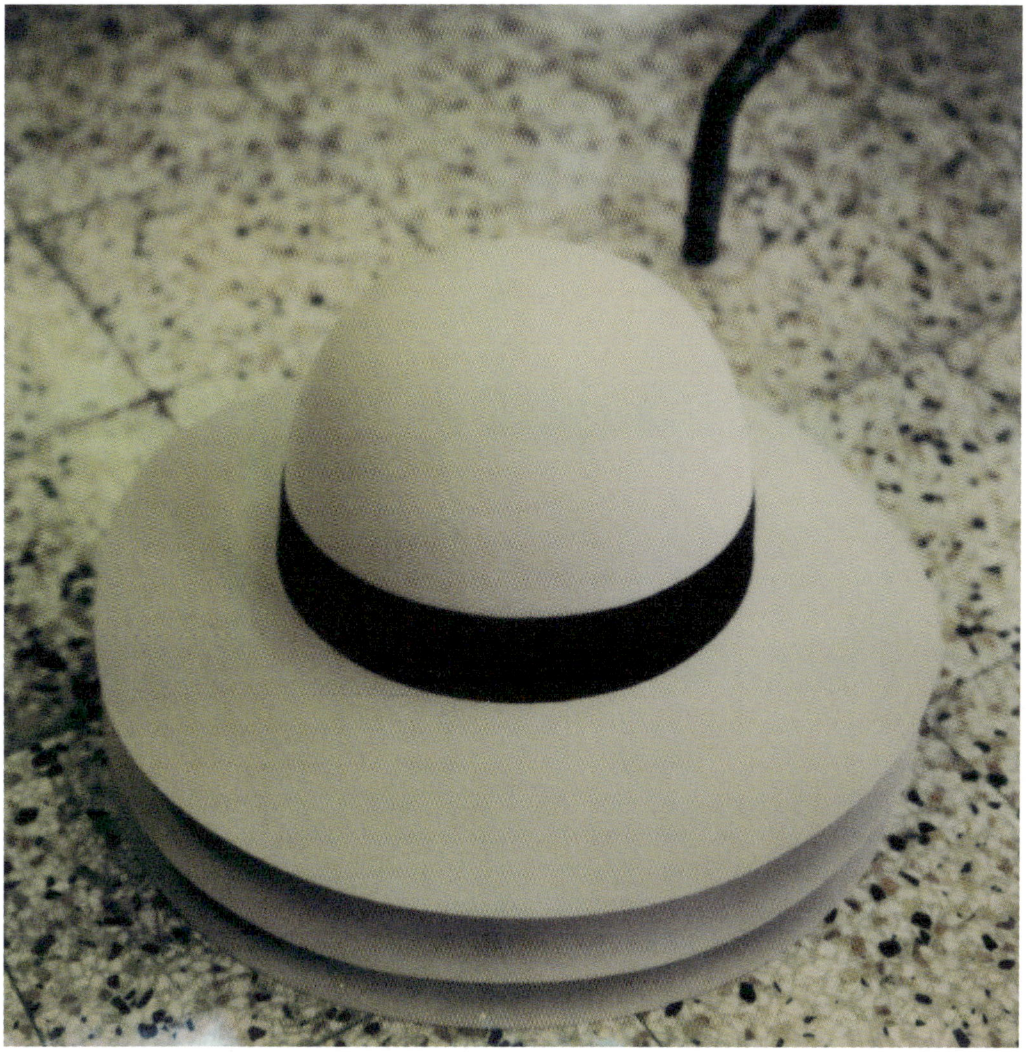

White felt hats on a grit floor

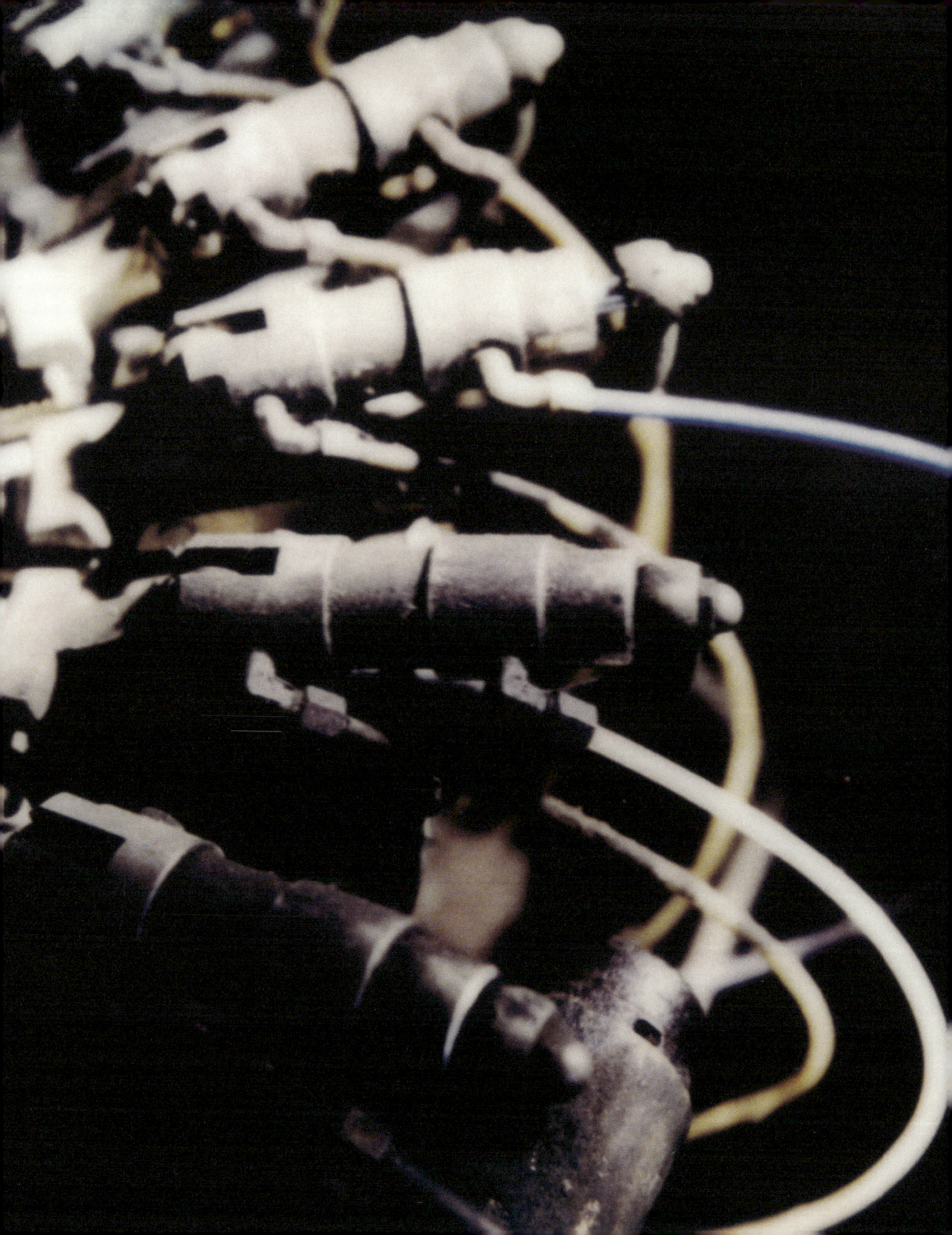

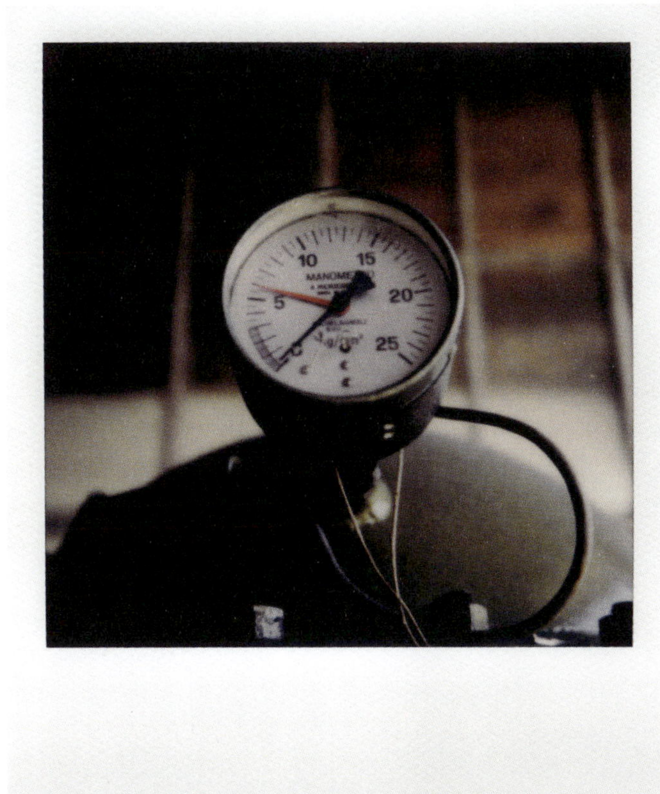
10
15
5
20
25

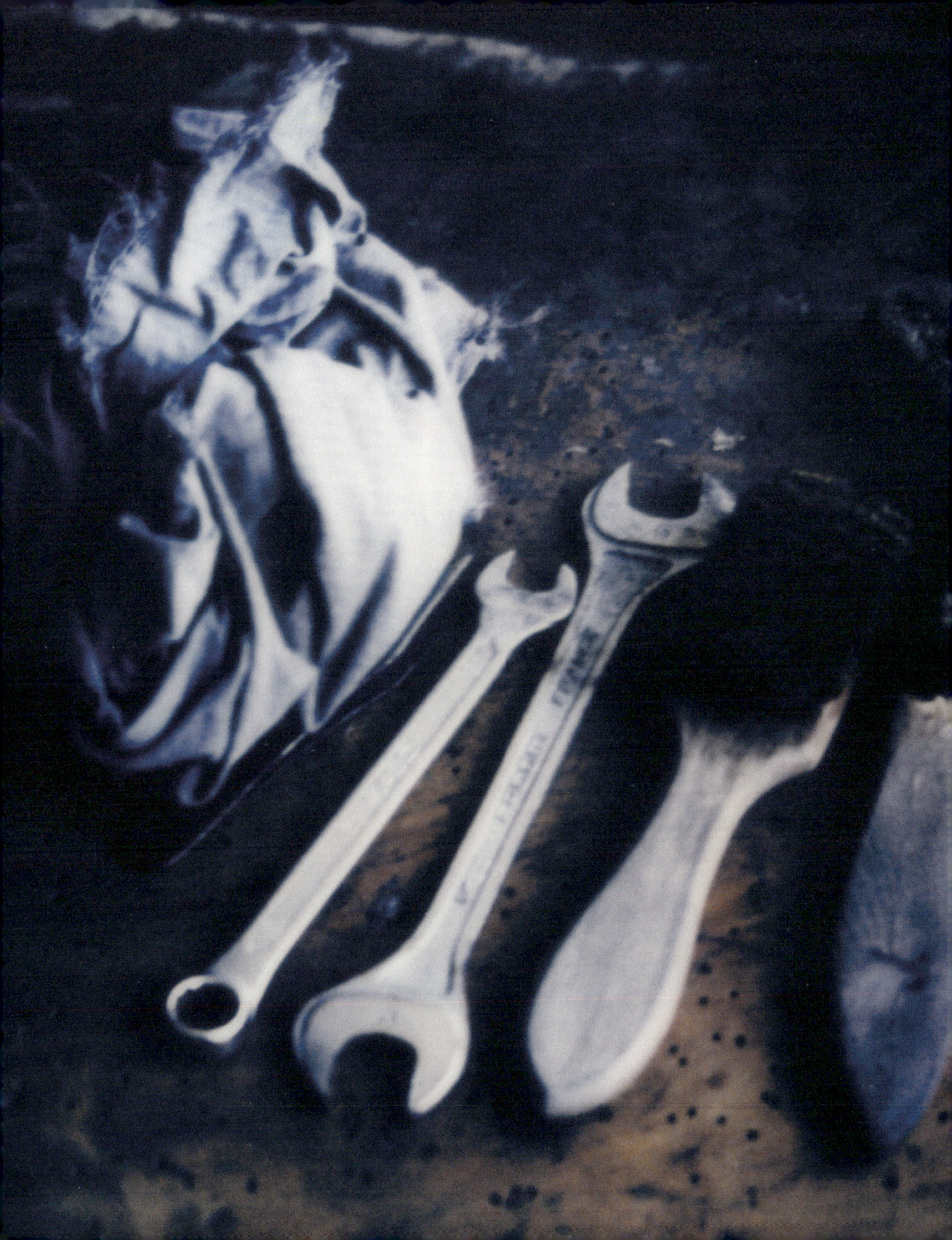

THE ART OF HAT-MAKING

ITALIAN CRAFTSMANSHIP FROM THE CERVO VALLEY

New Heroes & Pioneers

Published by New Heroes & Pioneers

Text and Photography: Giovanni Previdi
Creative Direction: Francois Le Bled
Book Design: Daniel Zachrisson
Copy Editing: Roxanne Sancto & Francois Le Bled

Print and bound by BALTO print (Lithuania)
Legal deposit November 2023
ISBN: 978-91-986566-7-1

FSC www.fsc.org MIX Paper from responsible sources FSC® C107574

With special thanks to Giorgio Borrione, Attilio Borrione, Benedetta Borrione, Veronica Borrione and to all the hatters at the Cappellificio Cervo who allowed me to document their precious art, making me feel like part of the family. To my publisher Francois Le Bled for having believed in this book from the start. To my father Mauro for lending me, many years ago, his film camera. And finally to my wife Silvia Avallone and my two little girls Nilde and Ingrid.

Behati on the move (opposite page)
Cappellificio Cervo (next spread)

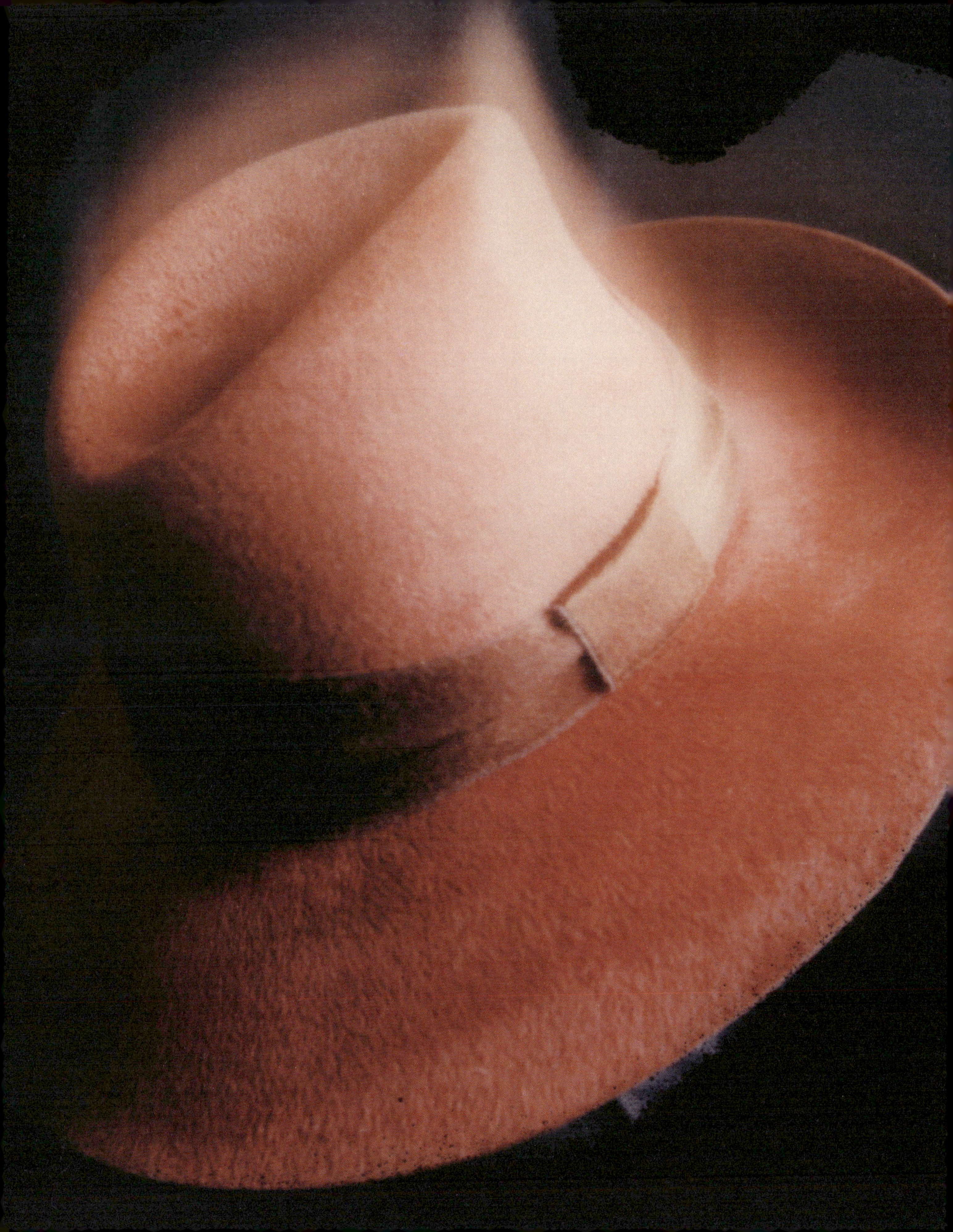

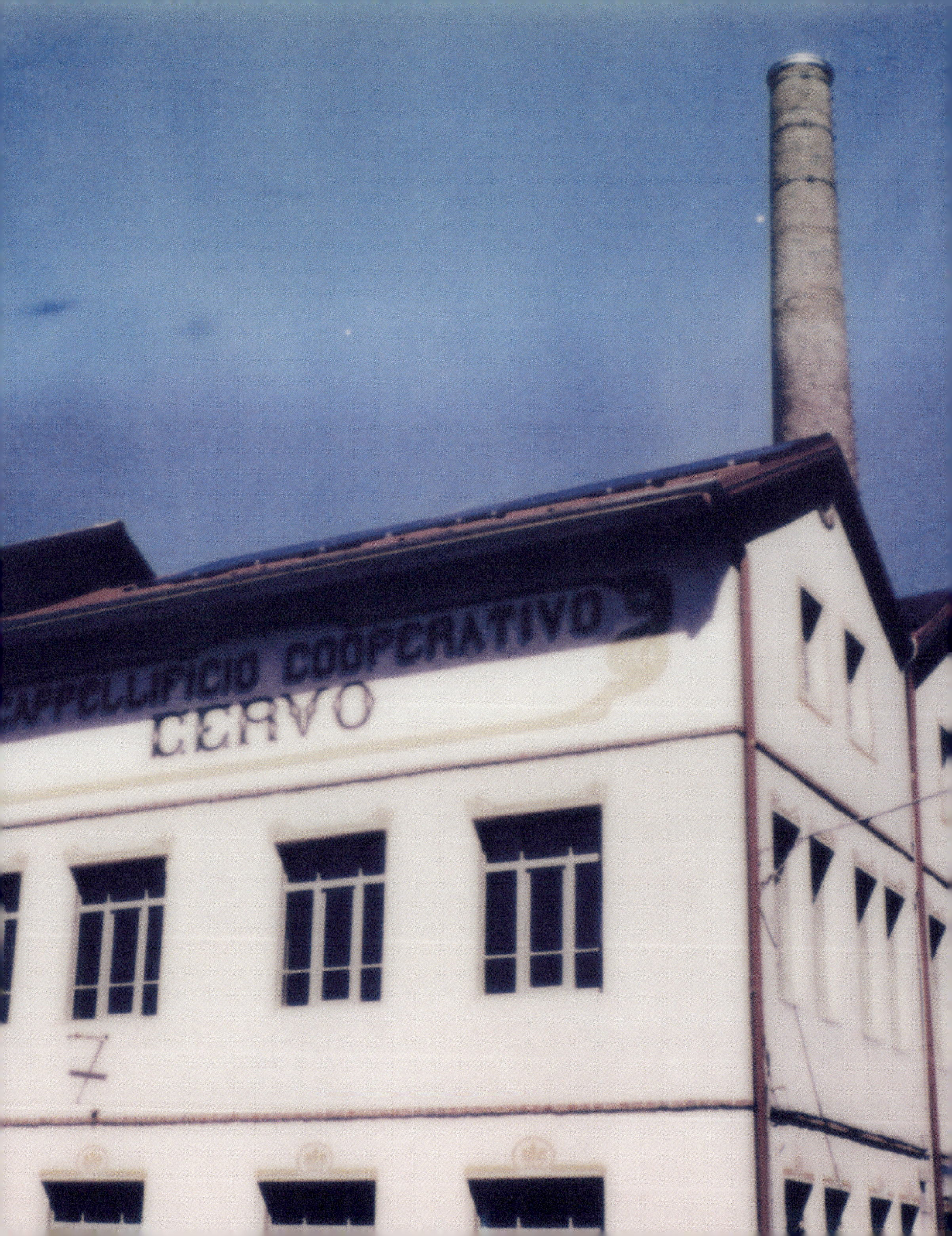
CAPPELLIFICIO COOPERATIVO
CERVO